THE POETRY OF TONY HARRISON

THE POETRY OF TONY HARRISON

Luke Spencer
University of Leeds

New York   London   Toronto   Sydney   Tokyo   Singapore

First published 1994 by
Harvester Wheatsheaf
Campus 400, Maylands Avenue
Hemel Hempstead
Hertfordshire, HP2 7EZ
A division of
Simon & Schuster International Group

Typeset in 10/12pt Plantin by
The Midlands Book Typesetting Company

Printed and bound in Great Britain by
Biddles Ltd, Guildford and King's Lynn

British Library Cataloguing in Publication Data

A catalogue record for this book is available from
the British Library

ISBN 0 7450 1588 3 (pbk)

1 2 3 4 5 98 97 96 95 94

FOR VAL

with love

Contents

Acknowledgements

The author and publisher are grateful to Tony Harrison and his publishers for permission to reproduce the following copyright material: extracts from *Earthworks* (Northern House Pamphlet Poets, 1964); extracts from *Palladas: Poems* (Anvil Press Poetry, 1975); extracts from *The Loiners* (London Magazine Editions, 1970); extracts from *The Misanthrope* (Rex Collings, 1973); extracts from *Selected Poems* (Penguin, 2nd edition, 1987); extracts from *Dramatic Verse 1973–1985* (Bloodaxe Books, 1985), *U.S. Martial* (Bloodaxe Books, 1981), and *The Gaze of the Gorgon* (Bloodaxe Books, 1992). Copyright in each of the above: Tony Harrison. Thanks are also due to Tony Harrison and to Faber & Faber Ltd for permission to quote extracts from *The Mysteries* (1985), *The Trackers of Oxyrhynchus* (1991), *The Common Chorus* (1992), and *Square Rounds* (1992).

I would like to thank Manchester University Press and the editors of *Literature and History* for permission to quote several paragraphs from an article of mine entitled ' "The grudge is true": working-class poetry in post-war Britain', which appeared in the Spring 1992 number of that journal. I would also like to thank the editors of *The Tempest*, Journal of the New Leeds Arts Club, for allowing me to reproduce, in a slightly modified form, my article on Tony Harrison's *v.* which appeared in their Launch Number in January 1993.

My editor at Simon & Schuster, Jackie Jones, has given me freely of her time, advice and encouragement, for all of which I am very grateful to her. Special thanks are due also to four colleagues:

ACKNOWLEDGEMENTS

Dick Taylor, for giving me study leave at exactly the right time; Jill Liddington, for sharing with me her considerable first-hand knowledge of the Greenham Women's camps; Ros Craggs, for making some shrewd comments on an early draft of what eventually became Chapter 5 below; and lastly Tom Steele, for many valuable conversations about contemporary writing during the last twenty years.

My wife, Valerie Spencer, deserves more thanks than I have room for here. I will mention only the good-humoured encouragement and unwavering critical interest with which she has supported me – sometimes at the expense of her own work – throughout the whole process of planning and writing (and worrying about) this book.

Preface

It is one of the greatest ironies of the current literary scene that the poetry of Tony Harrison should have become so familiar to so many people while receiving very little in the way of sustained critical attention. No doubt this can be partly accounted for by the intimidating scope and variety of that work – from sonnets and film-poems to plays and opera libretti. However, it is also because Harrison's upfront political concerns are ones with which only a few critics are willing to engage at any real depth of moral commitment or intellectual interest.

This book takes Harrison's social ideas as seriously as he does himself – and that means looking equally closely at the politics of his forms and the form of his politics. Only the closest attention to both these dimensions of his craft can help us take the measure of his achievement as one of the best political poets of this century.

Luke Spencer ·

Chronology

(With special emphasis on major publication, broadcasting and performance dates.)

1937   Harrison born on 30 April. Family home in Beeston Hill area of Leeds.

1948   wins scholarship from Cross Flatts Primary School to Leeds Grammar School.

1955   begins degree in Classics at Leeds University.

1958   awarded BA Hons. Begins PhD (not completed).

1962   awarded Postgraduate Diploma in English as a Second Language.

1962–6 lectures in English at Ahmadu Bello University, Nigeria. Here *Aikin Mata* (a version of *Lysistrata* by Harrison and James Simmons) performed in 1964.

1964   *Earthworks* published.

1966–7 teaches at Charles University, Prague.

1967–9 Northern Arts Literary Fellowship at Universities of Newcastle and Durham. Co-edits *Stand* magazine.

1969   'Newcastle is Peru' published as pamphlet by Eagle Press, Leeds. UNESCO Fellowship to Cuba, Brazil, Senegal and Gambia.

1970   *The Loiners* published.

1971   Six poems from *The Loiners* and one from *Earthworks* appear in *Corgi Modern Poets in Focus: 4*.

1973   *The Misanthrope* first performed and published (by Rex Collings, London).

1973–4   Gregynog Arts Fellowship, University of Wales.
1975   *Palladas: Poems* published. *Phaedra Britannica* performed and published. Writes lyrics for George Cukor's film version of Maeterlinck's play *The Blue Bird*.
1976–7   Northern Arts Literary Fellowship for second time.
1977   *Bow Down* performed at National Theatre and published by Rex Collings. *The Passion* (later Part Two of *The Mysteries*) published by Rex Collings.
1978   *From 'The School of Eloquence' and other poems* published.
1979–80   UK/US Bicentennial Fellowship at New York Metropolitan Opera House.
1981   Published: *Continuous* (Rex Collings); *A Kumquat for John Keats* (Bloodaxe); *U.S. Martial* (Bloodaxe). *The Oresteia* performed and published (Rex Collings). *Arctic Paradise* shown on BBC2 (first published in *Astley* 1991).
1984   First edition of *Selected Poems* published by Penguin.
1985   *The Mysteries* performed at National Theatre. Production filmed by Channel 4 and broadcast in December 1985 and January 1986. The full trilogy published by Faber. *Dramatic Verse 1973–1985* published by Bloodaxe. (Same text published by Penguin, with title *Theatre Works 1973–1985*, in 1986.) First edition of *v.* (Bloodaxe).
1986   *Yan Tan Tethera* (text written in 1983, to music by Harrison Birtwhistle) performed at Queen Elizabeth Hall. *Loving Memory*: four film-poems shown on BBC television.
1987   Second edition of *Selected Poems*. *Anno Forty-two* (Scargill Press). Recording of *Yan Tan Tethera* shown on Channel 4. Broadcast reading of *v.*
1987–8   President of Classical Association.
1988   *The Trackers of Oxyrhynchus* first performed at Delphi.
1989   Second edition of *v.*, with supplementary material from newspapers, etc.
1990   First edition of Delphi *Trackers* text (Faber). Revised version of the play performed at National Theatre.

1991   Second edition of *Trackers*, with Delphi and National
        Theatre texts. *A Cold Coming: Gulf War Poems*
        published by Bloodaxe. (Both poems appeared first in
        The Guardian.)

1992   *The Common Chorus* published by Faber, but still
        unperformed. *Square Rounds* performed at National
        Theatre and published by Faber. *The Gaze of the
        Gorgon* (Bloodaxe).

1993   BBC2 broadcast of *Black Daisies for the Bride*.
        Black Daisies for the Bride published by Faber.

Key to Abbreviations

Astley   Neil Astley (ed.), *Tony Harrison*, Bloodaxe Critical
Anthologies: 1, Bloodaxe Books, Newcastle upon Tyne,
1991.

CC   *The Common Chorus*, Faber & Faber, London, 1992.

DV   *Dramatic Verse 1973–1985*, Bloodaxe, Newcastle upon
Tyne, 1985. (See also *TW* below.)

E   *Earthworks*, Northern House Pamphlet Poets, Leeds,
1964.

GG   *The Gaze of the Gorgon*, Bloodaxe, Newcastle upon Tyne,
1992.

L   *The Loiners*, London Magazine Editions, London, 1970,
for all poems not in *SP*.

M   *The Mysteries*, Faber & Faber, London, 1985.

P   *Palladas: Poems*, Anvil Press Poetry, London, 1975.

SP   *Selected Poems*, second edition, Penguin,
Harmondsworth, 1987.

SR   *Square Rounds*, Faber & Faber, London, 1992.

TM   *The Misanthrope*, Rex Collings, London, 1973.

TO   *The Trackers of Oxyrhynchus*, Faber & Faber, London, 1991 edition.

TW   *Theatre Works 1973–1985*, Penguin, Harmondsworth, 1986. (This is in all major respects the same as *DV* above, including the page numbering.)

USM   *U.S. Martial*, Bloodaxe, Newcastle upon Tyne, 1981.

Of all titles, *v.* is the one that least requires – or allows – abbreviation. It is worth pointing out, however, that the second Bloodaxe edition (Newcastle upon Tyne, 1989) includes valuable extracts from media coverage of the row about the broadcasting of the poem. For the sake of continuity with the other chapters of this book, all quotations from *v.* are attributed to *Selected Poems* (1987).

Tony Harrison and working-class poetry in postwar Britain

The dead lie under our feet like pipelines.
(Douglas Dunn, 'The Local')

When Tony Harrison was interviewed by Richard Hoggart for ITV in 1986 it was a public get-together that many people had been looking forward to. In *The Uses of Literacy* (1957), Hoggart had long ago identified the personal and social factors that would make this meeting so appropriate for both men. In that pioneering study, Hoggart had drawn directly on his own Hunslet childhood and adolescence to describe the conflicts of loyalty felt by 'scholarship boys' like himself,[1] whose academic ability had attenuated to breaking-point their links with family, friends and community.[2] A generation before Harrison (who was born in 1937), Hoggart had won a scholarship from the local 'elementary' school to a grammar school and from there had gone to Leeds University to read English. Harrison's almost identical trajectory was via a scholarship to Leeds Grammar School ('the poshest school in town', according to Hoggart) to a Classics degree at the same university. Both suffered the isolation and growing alienation described in Hoggart's book and in some of Harrison's most moving 'School of Eloquence' sonnets (see pp. 75–7 below). Harrison's sense of fellow-feeling with Hoggart is wryly acknowledged in the dedication of 'Them & [uz]' to 'Professors Richard Hoggart & Leon Cortez'. Being thus coupled with a Cockney comic who debunked high culture no doubt contributed to Hoggart's pride in this dedication. It was obviously to be expected that the two men would have some interesting things to say to each other.

One of the least surprising things that the text of the interview reveals is an important respect in which Harrison is not like the *déclassé* plodder in Hoggart's thirty-year-old description:

> He begins to see life, for as far as he can envisage it, as a series of hurdle-jumps, the hurdles of scholarships which are won by learning how to amass and manipulate the new currency. He tends to over-stress the importance of examinations, of the piling-up of knowledge and of received opinions. He discovers a technique of apparent learning, of the acquiring of facts rather than the handling of facts. He learns how to receive a purely literate education, one using only a small part of the personality and challenging only a limited area of his being.[3]

Accurate as this is as a description of many thousands of products of a deeply divisive education system (and Dickens's Bradley Headstone is an earlier, more pathological specimen of the same sort of psychological damage), it is not at all like Tony Harrison or Hoggart himself. Instead of enduring a lifelong 'fear and shame of a possible falling-back'[4] into the working class, they have both been able to re-examine their backgrounds from the vantage point of maturity and worldly success, and to achieve greater understanding and a renewed feeling of solidarity in the process. This has meant facing up to many uncomfortable truths – about working-class narrowness as much as their own embourgeoisement; but they have been willing to do this in aid of what Harrison calls 'the reclamation of a life' that once seemed irrelevant to all that formal education was promoting.

Though the tensions of education versus class had a decisive impact on Hoggart and Harrison, they have both acknowledged the emotional support that was available to them in the family home at a formative stage of their lives. In the interview, Harrison even credits his mother with originating his interest in poetry: '. . . my love of rhyme, I think . . . came from that close family upbringing. Because my mother did tell me poems. . . . Nursery rhymes and things of that kind' (*Astley*, p. 40). In *The Uses of Literacy* Hoggart speculated about the long-term effect of spending a lot of time studying at home, 'in the women's world': 'Perhaps this partly explains why many authors from the working-classes, when they write about their childhood, give the women in it so tender and central a place.'[5] Hoggart was probably thinking mainly of Lawrence, but a number of later novelists would give support to his claim. Harrison's attitude is different. He tells Hoggart during their conversation that 'coming to terms with one's female qualities seems to be a very necessary struggle' (*Astley*, p. 45), but his work shows little tenderness towards women, his mother included. The reason for this may be something to do with what *The Uses of Literacy* hints at as the scholarship boy's compromised masculinity, the negative side of staying with the women:

> Such a scholarship boy has lost some of the resilience and some of the vitality of his cousins who are still knocking about the streets. In any earlier generation, as one of the quicker-witted persons born into the working-classes, he would in all probability have had these wits developed in the jungle of the slums, where wit had to ally itself to energy and initiative. . . . He loses something of the gamin's resilience and carelessness, of his readiness to take a chance, of his perkiness and boldness, and he does not acquire the unconscious confidence of many a public-school-trained child of the middle-classes.[6]

Whether the reference is to streetwise 'resilience', 'vitality' and 'boldness' or to middle-class 'confidence', the basic quality that is at issue here is masculinity. I do not mean to suggest that Harrison is a wimp. He is also, most emphatically, not the 'big man' who 'could be mistaken for a boxer' that Hoggart unaccountably claimed to have seen when interviewing him. (He is, in fact, short and lean.) What demands recognition, however, is that the sense of estrangement from his father and from other men haunts Harrison's poetry more prominently and persistently than any 'struggle' to come to terms with 'female qualities'. His face-off with the skinhead in *v.* reveals how far the skin's aggression is part of himself; his indulgence towards the rowdy squaddies in 'The Act' is prompted in part by his eagerness to insist that he also is one of the lads. Above all, his compulsion to find common ground on which he can meet and make peace with the memory of his father speaks of a powerful need for male acceptance and approval.

If working-class scholars were bound to come up against problems of alienation and identity, there was an additional twist

3

to the dilemma reserved for those who wanted to write about their class experience. George Orwell pointed this out in a 1940 radio interview: 'Proletarian literature is mainly a literature of revolt. It can't help being so.'[7] However, 'so long as the bourgeoisie are the dominant class, literature must be bourgeois'.[8] Orwell could not envisage much more than a limited oppositional role for proletarian writing, for two main reasons: first, because he thought English society was becoming classless, and that therefore the proletarian writer would soon have nothing specifically working-class to write (i.e. protest) about; second, because until the hegemony of bourgeois culture ended, the proletarian writer could do little more than add a working-class inflection to still-dominant bourgeois forms: 'He is simply the black sheep of the bourgeois family, using the old methods for slightly different purposes.'[9] Orwell's confident wartime vision of a classless Britain (or England, at least) obviously failed to materialise[10], which left his second proposition as a more enduring predicament than he envisaged. To be sure, middle-class (and white, male, heterosexual) attitudes turned out to be much more resilient than Orwell could have anticipated. Yet, at the same time, oppositional voices showed themselves to be more versatile and less easily assimilated than Orwell's view allowed for. This happened in some measure because class ceased to be the single focus of opposition. A range of subcultural groups that often crossed and recrossed traditional class divisions put many long-neglected issues on the cultural-political agenda – issues of race, gender, sexuality and national/regional identity. Nevertheless, identifiably working-class issues and perspectives remained a central concern for many writers – most obviously in the novel, less so in the theatre and in only a few significant instances in what got widely published and reviewed as 'poetry'.[11] Just where working-class writing, and Tony Harrison's work in particular, can be located on the map of postwar British poetry is the concern of what follows.

In 1977 Eric Homberger identified what he saw as an acute malaise afflicting English and American poetry: 'We have gone into a period of the most severe privatization of meaningful experience, and there is no knowing how long this cultural vacuum is going to last. It seems unlikely that important literature is going to come out of it.'[12] This looks especially perceptive if we remember the scriptural importance that 'privatization' was to be given by the outcome of the 1979 general election in Britain. The self-aggrandising materialism promoted by the first Thatcher government, and with increasing ferocity by its successors, was an apotheosis of the very cultural tendencies remarked by Homberger. In the world that so soon came to be typified by the political success and mutual admiration of Thatcher in Britain and Reagan in the United States, poetry's rapt attention to personal experience invariably precluded any reference to social, let alone explicitly political, issues. It was as though most poets were instinctively subscribing to Mrs Thatcher's notorious maxim 'There is no such thing as society'. In only a very few cases was significant poetry produced that did not totally ignore the 'real' in Homberger's sense – that is to say, 'contingent values, other people, history itself'.[13]

The difficulty of trying to find a way back to a more public position for poetry in the teeth of such opposition is well illustrated by Jon Silkin's *Poetry of the Committed Individual* (1973), an anthology drawn from twenty years of *Stand* magazine and faithfully reflecting that journal's inclusive interests, especially in non-English poets. In his introduction, Silkin wrestles with the problem of how to bring social commitment back through the front door without sacrificing either what he calls 'the essentiality of the poet's impulse' or such vital elements of formal integrity as conciseness and enactment.[14] Despite such good intentions, the anthology lives up to its title mainly through the work of poets from Eastern Europe and beyond. Only a handful of the British poets represented can bear comparison with the likes of Nazim Hikmet or Zbigniew Herbert. One of them is Tony Harrison, who co-edited *Stand* in the late 1960s, when a Northern Arts Literary Fellowship first brought him to Newcastle.

By the time Silkin's anthology was published, the two most popular substitutes for a social perspective in British poetry were either Philip Larkin's disdainful digs at the welfare state or Ted Hughes's anti-humanitarian primitivism. Larkin in particular provided a direct link with the 1950s, when 1930s-style political engagement and the neo-Romanticism of the 1940s were both alike rejected in favour of what, in 1957, *New Lines* regarded as more honest, more intellectually rigorous poetry freed from both 'great systems of theoretical constructs' (i.e. Marxism) on the one hand and 'agglomerations of unconscious commands' (i.e. Surrealism and neo-Romanticism) on the other.[15] Such a return to the would-be innocent empiricism of the British philosophical tradition was by no means incompatible with the darker forces celebrated by Hughes.[16] Both were equally safe politically: Hughes provided a taste of blood and guts to season the insular 'gentility' that was the stock in trade of Larkin and other Movement poets.[17] That Larkin should eventually declare himself an ardent Thatcherite and that Hughes, as Poet Laureate, should end up providing bespoke commemorative verses for royal births and marriages (though not yet any separations or divorces) now seems entirely appropriate. The Homberger passage quoted above was written too early to take account of either outcome, but it anticipates them in its anxiety about the absence of a discernible alternative to the entrenched inwardness which, by the late 1970s, blocked the way to a properly social perspective for poetry.

Two years before Homberger's book appeared, the Scottish working-class poet Douglas Dunn wrote an editorial for *Stand* called 'The Grudge'.[18] In it he argued that the special predicament of a working-class writer like himself is that 'His work is . . . directed at an audience who do not receive it; instead, it is received by an audience of those he is against.'[19] Dunn was able to acknowledge, as Orwell had done thirty years before, both the oppositional imperative of working-class writing and the inescapable dilemma posed for it by bourgeois cultural dominance. The best way of negotiating that dilemma, Dunn argued, is 'commitment . . . the idea under which a working-class poet can organise the sundry circumstances which belong to him and which cohere in the form of beliefs about the world'.[20] This offers genuine hope of bringing poetry into a mutually beneficial relationship to politics; of enabling the poet to 'see poetry as the vision of its own classless society'.[21] Moreover, such a vision fosters resentment – a grudge – towards those who have relegated poetry to an instrument of their own class ascendancy. Therefore, it is necessary to keep that grudge intact: its purity will help to prevent the dilution and assimilation of the working-class poet's emancipatory project.

It was by learning to make creative use of their grudge that Dunn and Harrison have proved to be the most successful of working-class poets in supplying the kind of social perspective (or 'art of the real') demanded by Homberger. Other poets from similar backgrounds have abandoned class-related poetry for intense meditations on their personal lives (e.g. Tony Connor), or they have developed a species of social perspective outside of poetry, as Glyn Hughes has done in a recent trilogy of historical novels.[22] In the case of Craig Raine there is an obvious ability to write with great precision about his working-class upbringing (as in 'A Silver Plate', the central – and, significantly, prose – section of *Rich* (1984)), but also a firm refusal to allow a class perspective to cloud the special (Martian) brand of empiricism which he has made his own.

The Liverpool poets, in particular Roger McGough, have produced some sharp-edged observations of working-class life; but their poetry remains limited by its preoccupation with the whimsicality of urban existence, rather than its all-too-real injustices. (In contrast, the 'protest' poetry of Adrian Mitchell originates directly from his courageous ideological opposition to Western capitalism and imperialism, but not from any first-hand experience – as victim, at least – of class subordination.) Tom Pickard has drawn on Tyneside speech to dramatise the brutality of proletarian male attitudes and to expose the indignities of unemployment. Unfortunately, his poetry has generally been slackly self-indulgent in both form and intellectual content. Among women poets a distinctively working-class voice is hard to find, though their understandable concern with gender issues must sooner or later be related to class, if only in order to confront traditional socialist or Labourist phallocentrism. (I look forward to someone producing an anthology by, for example, the members of the Women Against Pit Closures organisation.)

Of course, an enormous amount of valuable work is produced by working-class women (and men) in creative writing classes and arts groups of all kinds. That work may be read and circulated only within a small group of people; or it may be published in one of the many little magazines that testify to an abiding strength of interest in poetry as a means of self-expression and communal dialogue. At the other end of the public visibility scale there is pop culture and John Lennon's 'Working-Class Hero' as an example of how forcefully a class perspective can be articulated in a rock-music context.

Like Douglas Dunn, Tony Harrison took time to organise the scattered humiliations and resentments of his early years into a grudge coherent enough to give shape and direction to his poetry. In his case, this process was to include not only a refinement of his class perspective but also – as an integral feature of such emergent radicalism – a developing (though not always evenly developing,

7

as I shall show) political view of sexuality, colonialism and state repression. The time he spent away from England gave a huge impetus to this widening of his political horizons. His stint of lecturing in Nigeria (1962–6) extended his already considerable knowledge of languages, but it also gave him an inside view of the impact of colonialism that contributed greatly to the anarchic anger of *The Loiners*. His year in Prague (1966–7) introduced him at first hand to the realities of state surveillance, and helped to consolidate the commitment to freedom of expression that burns so fiercely in later work like 'The Blasphemers' Banquet'. In 1969 a UNESCO Fellowship took him to Cuba, among other places, and there he witnessed the struggle to sustain a revolution on lines very different from the sclerosis of Eastern Europe. If individual creativity could be threatened by the state (as in Czechoslovakia), there were also ways in which it might be encouraged as part of a project of *collective* emancipation – from illiteracy, poverty and centuries-old exploitation. Here, as much as in Harrison's reading of Edward Thompson, lay the seeds of libertarian socialism that would grow into the earliest 'School of Eloquence' sonnets.

While Harrison was in Nigeria, his first collection of poems – nine altogether – was published in the 'Northern House Pamphlet Poets' series (1964). Its title, *Earthworks*, bluntly announces its anti-metaphysical, feet-on-the-ground source of inspiration. Through the formal regularities that he is already relying on to support some disturbing explorations, Harrison reverts constantly to the leitmotiv of earth/land. The opening poem is a six-line rejection of the consolations of religion in which one land, a 'fertile, golden . . . El Dorado', is swapped for the 'cold snow' of the North by the migratory imagination. Even though it is handicapped ('crippled') by religious belief, the imagination can still find the strength to escape to the world of other people (and other poets), shitting in God's hand as a farewell gesture of emancipation. The 'wet guano' thus deposited would, of course, make a uniquely fertile soil in which anything and everything might grow.

Growth of a less creative sort is the theme of 'The Hybrid Growth'. In it a dying woman is surrounded by roses like those she has spent her life cultivating. It is as though her own life has itself been cultivated by death for the plucking that is now imminent. Her family fill her room with 'choicest heads', their own and those of the cut flowers. They hope the roses will somehow keep the woman's death at bay (by rekindling her interest in life, as tulips did for Sylvia Plath?). The woman herself puts her faith in a sort of rebirth (not necessarily a spiritual one) whereby her heart will 'open out' again, and the drooping roses will become 'horns' sounding her transfiguration (as spirit, or simply as recycled matter?). Her garden has been an 'ordered world' in which roses' growth and decay have symbolised for her the inevitability of death. Mortality is a failure to keep pace with time, which, like a hybrid growth forever revitalising itself, inexorably outlasts all forms of earthly life. Because death subsists on 'fumes' much less substantial ('lighter') than the scent of life, it can move more freely 'through the world', though (it is implied) with none of life's earthbound intensity either. This poem is itself a not very hardy hybridisation of woman and rose, 'gardener and growth'. The most striking thing that emerges from its laboured conceits is that Keatsian hunger for time-bound sensuous pleasure that culminated in the offered 'Kumquat' seventeen years later.

Another, but more successful, use of the rose image is in 'The Promised Land', where the woman's unnatural withdrawal from the world is partly represented by the 'perfect rose' on her carpet, which she prefers to the real, perishable thing outside. Her bastion is a self-sustaining one in which the flowered carpet, 'manure[d]' by her life and able to absorb the petty accidents of quotidian existence, figures her substitution of a parody of life for the genuine article. Her promised land, like the religionists' El Dorado in the earlier poem, is a denial of promise; it is an enclave of manicured domesticity, with its pampered cat as a substitute for human marital and parental love. To the male onlooker, this is nothing at all to do with genuine love:

> Love must be made like houses, or
>   Like her contented cat
>   Be shown the door,
>
> To find outside the reason why
> It has no right to purr like that.
>   (*E*, p. 9)

The poem's epigraph, from the Book of Hosea, speaks of bringing a woman into the wilderness and offering her emotional support while

9

she faces worldly reality. Because the man in the poem is unable to do the first thing, he never gets a chance to do the second.

The main reality which the poems' down-to-earthness confronts is the failure of a heterosexual relationship, probably a marriage, to overcome a sense of separation and lack of mutual support. 'The New Earth' deals movingly with the death of a newborn child, a 'clod of birth' immediately reclaimed as a piece of inanimate matter. New earth/new birth; ashes to ashes, dust to dust: the enormity of the stillbirth and its consoling ordinariness in the scheme of things are perfectly balanced in the poem's two four-line stanzas.

'The Flat Dweller's Revolt' takes a look at the emotional cost of this bereavement. The male flat dweller who goes for a walk to escape the entrapment of 'claustrophobic voices' and 'suffocated talk' meditates on 'the fruitless [both childless and unrewarding] dark'. The seeds of the plants he kicks are free to spread and grow; he hopes that in what is, for them, a 'fallow night', willowherb will spring up vigorously among the carefully cultivated garden plants, as if to assert the right to life of 'unwanted children'. The 'common earth', where such weeds might spread, is also where men like himself, as putative fathers or 'ageing sons', are forced to recognise the transience of life and the (implied) need to procreate. The 'flesh and bone' which the man calls forth in learning himself 'by heart' are his own human substance, his family ties and what he hopes to create out of himself, despite the woman's reluctance to have another child after the stillbirth of their first.

In the last stanza, after returning to the flat, the man longs for the moon ('queen' of tides and the ebb and flow of women's moods) to break the defences ('dykes') of 'protected brides' and flood their fertile wombs – presumably with fertilising sperm. This is a very early example of a masculinity whose self-absorption is given free rein in determining the shape and substance of the poem. The woman is a shadowy background figure who, in the absence of more than a hint about the death of the first child ('one birth/ . . . one stone'), ends up embodying stereotypical female stubbornness and sexual non-compliance. The only solution to this situation that the man can imagine is one in which every bride's defences will simply be overwhelmed in a sort of divinely sanctioned elemental gang-bang.

Futile sexual effort is the theme of 'The Pathetic Fallacy' (with a pun on 'phallus-y') and 'The Hands'. The first of these represents two people's coupling in a hotel room as simply a transfer of sperm ('dark seed'), part of a joyless, haphazard post-lapsarian 'infestation' that mechanically renews life each spring. If April is not the cruellest month, it is certainly a pretty squalid one. In 'The Hands', earth-imagery is hardly present at all; but the poem is an ingenious figuring of sexual struggle as a pair of hands tentatively exploring, seeking a hold, missing their grip and finally sinking in a canal as a last, suicidal admission of defeat.

Apart from 'The New Earth', the poems in which the earth/land leitmotiv works best are 'The Pit of Perception' and 'A Part of the Mainland: Bardsey Island'. The pit of the first title is a building site on which trees have been bulldozed out of the ground to make way for house foundations. A bonfire of unwanted wood transfigures the surroundings, turning them into a primal scene of earth formation. Human social life is suddenly, startlingly seen as a frantic evolutionary struggle among micro-organisms, and the final image is that of the earth 'turned up again' to reveal a tangle of projecting branches grimly parodying human bones. The pit (nadir) of perception is thus one from which human life appears nasty, brutish and short. The play on roots and bones recalls Thom Gunn's unsettled motorcyclist (in 'The Unsettled Motorcyclist's Vision of his Death', *The Sense of Movement* (1957)), though Harrison offers nothing like the biker's existentialist bravado in the face of nature's inexorable processes.

The 'Bardsey Island' poem is an early venture into the sixteen-line form of 'The School of Eloquence', but without rhyme. It opens with an image of buried saints as an integral ingredient of the island's earth. Their 'sanctity' has been absorbed by every inch of animate and inanimate nature. Even God 'wallows in the pigsties', dispersed in spirit ('Wild holiness') throughout his creation. Or at least that's the way the Welsh religious enthusiasts very nationalistically see it. Others 'might note' a horde of demons exactly equal in number to the twenty thousand saints, and 'not Welsh' either, as a Manichaean antidote to the believers' fanaticism. The paradoxical attachment of Bardsey 'Island' to the mainland, foregrounded in the poem's title, is a trope for the existential realities with which even the most zealous otherworldliness and exclusivity must sooner or later come to terms.

Earth images are prominent in Harrison's work for several reasons. They are evidence of his commitment to the things of this world, his refusal to look beyond it. They also register the development of his concern with how what is most personal is at the same time rooted in specific local and communal experience:

> Ploughed parallel as print the stony earth.
> The straight stone walls defy the steep grey slopes.
> The place's rightness for my mother's birth
> exceeds the pilgrim grandson's wildest hopes –
>
> (*SP*, p. 177)

This stanza (the first) from 'Lines to my Grandfathers, I' is unlike anything in *Earthworks*. It represents the earth as not only material and this-worldly, but also as a site of human labour, marked by the furrows and dry-stone walls that testify to unremitting struggle, and to a careful craft that is a kind of communal writing ('print'), the signature of the historically silent. Earth as the object and arena of such effort is a trope which also links the sonnets that deal with those whose labour was beneath the ground, the miners of 'Working' and 'National Trust'. And it takes on a further dimension in some of the American poems, where the flora and ˙ fauna of Florida represent a natural world still full of richness and surprise despite human depredations.

In the first volume of his autobiography, Richard Hoggart lists five qualities of his character and outlook that were firmly established during his early years in Leeds. The fourth of these is useful in defining one dimension of the working-class writer's response to his or her background. Hoggart stresses:

> the need to gain respect and by my own efforts. Which seems to be above all by writing, not by professional positions attained or by making money. By writing, for respect; but not only for the respect of others; even more, for self-respect. And for more than that – because of the conviction that this is how you may begin to get hold of your life, make more sense of it, in some way command it or at least understand it better; so no activity is more testing and in the end more enjoyable.[23]

As an honest statement of the need to make sense of one's life by thought and effort, this is completely convincing. It fits well with the very personal tone and emphasis of Hoggart's work. From *The Uses of Literacy* onwards there has been an unmistakable and characteristic registering of things on his own pulses. At its worst this emphasis produces mere anecdote and chat. At its best it conveys very strongly the sense of an earnest intelligence tracing its own alert passage through the contemporary world. Tony Harrison's work frequently shares with Hoggart's this positioning of the reflective self centre-stage. However, there is a further dimension to Harrison's work, one which he shares with Raymond Williams, another writer from a working-class family. Of his own writing, Williams says:

> whenever I write I am aware of a society and of a language which I know are vastly larger than myself: not simply 'out there' in a world of others, but here, in what I am engaged in doing: composing and relating. And if this is so at what can be seen as one end of the process, it seems to be equally true at the other: what is usually defined as what we are 'writing about'. . . . Even the ideas and experiences you think you are taking to the page come out differently, again and again, as you go through the actual practice, which is one of intense and locally isolated concentration and yet, at the same time, as I have experienced it, a condition of active presence – assisting and resisting – of the wider forces of a language and a society.[24]

Like Hoggart, Williams is concerned with the difficult business of 'composing and relating' his own 'ideas and experiences'; but his perspective is crucially different with regard to cultural influences. There is, for Williams, an intimate interaction going on all the time between private and public experience. This takes place above all through language which is a social product that must be constantly reproduced (and, if possible, renovated) in personal discourse. Ideologically speaking, Williams's position is collectivist and socialist, Hoggart's individualist and liberal. It is not that Hoggart is indifferent to society, or that Williams undervalues what is authentic about the 'personal': since the 1950s both men

13

have deservedly had an enormous influence on the development
of cultural studies as an academic subject and, more importantly,
as a methodology combining traditional disciplines and congenial
to new thinking. Together they help to demarcate two emphases
which sometimes complement and are sometimes at odds with each
other in the poetry that is the subject of this book.

Tony Harrison has himself offered plenty of comments on where he
thinks his work should be placed on the personal–social, biographical–
historical axis. When he speaks of his use of italics in 'The School
of Eloquence', it is the social and historical end of the scale that he
has most in mind:

> It seemed as if the *italic* could somehow take over from the
> *roman* – I mean a pun on *roman*, since what I designate in
> *roman* type in the poems is me as the poet – so that in the
> end I could become a mouthpiece. In the end, that is to
> say, there could be poems which are all italics.
>
> (Interview with John Haffenden, *Astley*, p. 229)

Writing for the stage is one way Harrison has found of giving
a voice to other people; but what his best non-theatre work
achieves is a dialectic of self and society (roman and italic)
which acknowledges, as completely as the Williams passage, the
reciprocity of the two.

One of the two major arguments of this study is that Harrison's
poetry achieves most, both ideologically and aesthetically, when it
is most open to, and most ready to foreground, the social and
historical dimensions of experience. This openness has occurred
most effectively in respect of his own class background and what
he has recognised as his inheritance of generations-old repression
and resistance. It has also contributed vitally to the oppositional
attitudes to be found throughout his work – those towards, among
other things, colonialism, imperialism, militarism, consumerism
and organised intolerance of all kinds. The other major argument
is that Harrison's class perspective (his 'grudge') is not adequate
for a full recognition of where gender properly belongs among
the ideological constraints and sites of contestation to which a
thoroughgoing radicalism must address itself. Why there should
be so many instances of misunderstanding, hostility or well-meant

condescension towards women in his work and so little empathy or real respect for them is a question that can be adequately dealt with only in a larger cultural and political context, and a more exhaustive biographical one, than is possible here. Nevertheless, it is important to identify the *consequences* of such a masculine political limitation, not least because its presence continually throws into sharper relief Harrison's substantial insights into many other areas of social reality. He himself has implicitly endorsed such a critical procedure by acknowledging the challenge – even the affront – offered by his poetry: 'I know that people who like some parts of my work are discomfited by other parts, and that's no bad thing' (Haffenden interview, *Astley*, p. 246). Registering 'discomfiture', as well as agreement and praise, is an indispensable part of one's dialogue with texts, especially those of a writer as courageously partisan and self-revealing as Harrison.

READING THE METRE

Harrison has described his contribution to the National Theatre production of *The Mysteries* as that of 'a Yorkshire poet who came to read the metre' (Preface to *M*). This mock self-deprecation wittily identifies three crucial features of his work: its North of England, working-class origins and inspiration; its dogged attention to an often repetitive, but indispensable job of work; its heavy reliance on 'traditional' formal procedures. Though the remark refers most immediately to his eagerness to preserve the metrical (and other technical) characteristics of the original pageant-play cycles, it can stand without modification as a statement of the formal strategy that shapes all his work. Rightly renowned as an inventor of ingenious rhymes, Harrison is also enormously resourceful in his appropriations of a huge range of poetic structures, from the variously rhymed paragraphs of *The Loiners* and most of the plays to Meredithian sonnets and quatrains in the manner of Thomas Gray and Omar Khayyam. His immense skill in these areas is discussed and illustrated at length in the chapters that follow. However, his use of metre requires some detailed preliminary attention – partly because scanning Harrison's lines is a complicated business, but more importantly because it is on the rhythmic bedrock of English prosody, especially the iambic

15

foot, that Harrison has fought many of his toughest ideological and aesthetic battles.

> An urbane severity hardens Harrison's poetry, tenses the frame of his metre, which is vigorous in playing off its classicism against a demotic Leeds background.
>
> (*Astley*, p. 255)

Coming as it does from a master technician like Douglas Dunn, this comment is a good place to begin an assessment of Harrison's metrical achievements. Elsewhere in the same lecture Dunn invokes a string of relevant literary influences and comparisons (Virgil, Juvenal, Dryden, Gray) in identifying Harrison's 'classic obedience to lucidity' (*Astley*, p. 257). But Dunn is not the sort of writer to ignore the ideological dimension of the poetry: he notes that it is 'Often . . . oppositional to orthodox social expectations'. Harrison himself makes a similar link between restraint and the challenge to orthodoxy when he describes metre as being for him 'an existential need' and, crucially, 'like a life-support system. It means I feel I can go close to the fire, deeper into the darkness' (*Astley*, p. 43). If Harrison intended a glance towards Conrad's Kurtz here, it is an appropriate one, for Kurtz was defeated by a lack of restraint when he came face to face with manifest social injustice in the shape of imperialism. One aspect of – or, at least, a valid substitute for – restraint in Conrad's *Heart of Darkness* is work, with its dependable routines and minor civilities. Though Harrison uses a more organic image – that of a 'pulse' – to describe the metrical underpinning of his poetry, there is also the strong suggestion of a sanity-saving craft, like that of seamanship. Art as the means of facing the otherwise unfaceable (unimaginable; intolerable) is a familiar formulation.

Nevertheless, the major problem for a self-consciously proletarian writer like Harrison is not so much how to face the 'darkness' of social and psychic suffering, but how (returning to Orwell) to fashion truly oppositional meanings out of fundamentally bourgeois establishment poetic forms. (Again there is a parallel with *Heart of Darkness* here; for the very work that saves the sanity of individuals may, like that of the Company's chief accountant, be thoroughly complicit with the larger social structures and objectives of the prevailing 'madness'.) In relation to the dominance of the iambic pentameter in English poetry, this problem cannot be overstated. Its scale is clearly suggested by some comments of Antony Easthope:

> Unruffled smoothness, flowing elegance, poise: these are qualities the counterpoint of pentameter [i.e. regular alternation of unstressed and stressed syllables] facilitates in two respects. Through counterpoint the abstract pattern of the metre is relatively backgrounded. Recognition of the work of metric *production* – and so of the poem as constructed artifice – is suppressed in favour of a notion of the poem as spontaneously generated *product*. . . . Pentameter makes verse especially compatible with the 'Received Pronunciation' of Standard English (the bourgeois norm). It does so because it legislates for the number of syllables in the line and therefore cancels elision, making transition at word junctures difficult. . . . Such pronunciation – one thinks of Laurence Olivier – signals 'proper' speech; that is, a class dialect.[25]

What Easthope says of the iambic pentameter (a five-foot line) can be said to some extent of other iambic lines, the point being that the iambic foot allows the optimum combination of classical (Greek and Latin) binary metrical order with the rhythms and pronunciation patterns of a hegemonic 'class dialect'. Harrison's work shares with the bulk of English poetry its reliance on the iambic foot. From *The Loiners* onwards he has found many ways of disturbing its 'unruffled smoothness', and of marshalling its energies in lines as short as two syllables and as long as fifteen. But the work of resistance, subversion and appropriation is never-ending, for there is always danger in a metre that can so minimise the reality of work and struggle ('production') while blandly endorsing the very Received Pronunciation (RP) that has been ruthlessly imposed upon, or used to exclude, generations of working-class schoolchildren who could not pronounce poetry 'correctly'.

When, in 'Them & [uz]', Harrison resolves to 'occupy/your lousy leasehold Poetry' (*SP*, p. 123), he is beginning a lifetime's battle to make the regularity of iambic metre yield to the unmannerly interruption of a subaltern voice. That voice is most strident in *v.*:

So what's a cri-de-coeur, *cunt? Can't you speak*
the language that yer mam spoke. Think of 'er!
Can yer only get yer tongue round fucking Greek?
Go and fuck yerself with cri-de-coeur!

(*SP*, p. 241)

The battle – a formal dialectic to match the clash of attitudes – is waged line by line, with the iambic pattern made to buckle and bend under the onslaught of the skinhead's anger. Only the second line is regular, its even rhythm a simultaneous enactment of the skinhead's class loyalty (with a touch of 'dear old mum' sentiment thrown in?) and an ironic reminder of the well-bred discourse he elsewhere scorns. In line 1 the full weight of his metrical vandalism falls on 'cunt', one of several obscenities widely deployed as metre-raiders as well as lexical bovver-boots. Where an unstressed syllable is anticipated, we get a word that not only requires a full stress but mugs us with the ferocity of its scorn. Line 3 begins with a stress that adds an extra syllable to what would have been a regular pentameter, underscoring the skinhead's difficulty with, and dislike of, 'fucking Greek'. The last line's initial stress is weaker than this, but its disruptive impact is as strong, especially in a line that comes out at a crippled nine syllables – that is, the initial stress followed by only four iambic feet (a tetrameter).

Easthope speaks of the pentameter's resistance both to 'elision' and to 'transition at word junctures' as aspects of its privileging of RP. Harrison's counter-strategy is brilliantly demonstrated in 'The Queen's English':

Last meal together, Leeds, the Queen's Hotel,
that grandish pile of swank in City Square.
Too posh for me! he said (though he dressed well)
If you weren't wi' me now ah'd nivver dare!

I knew that he'd decided that he'd die
not by the way he lingered in the bar,
nor by that look he'd give with one good eye,
nor the firmer handshake and the gruff *ta-ra*,
but when we browsed the station bookstall sales
he picked up *Poems from the Yorkshire Dales* –

'ere tek this un wi'yer to New York
to remind yer 'ow us gaffers used to talk.
It's up your street in't it? ah'll buy yer that!

The broken lines go through me speeding South –
As't Doctor stopped to oppen woodland yat . . .
and
　　wi'skill they putten wuds reet i'his mouth.

(*SP*, p. 136)

I count thirteen elisions in sixteen lines here, all but three of them belonging either to the italicised speech of Harrison's father or to the quoted lines of the dialect verse. The contrast between the 'swank' of the Queen's Hotel and the father's lack of social confidence is carried over into the difference between the poem's conventional poetic structure and the awkward presence within it of the father's demotic voice. Harrison's predicament, as educated poet and loyal son, is represented by the pull of his own colloquialisms and elisions against the metrical smoothness and faultless masculine rhymes: 'that grandish pile of swank in City Square' has all these elements in a perfect counterpoise of contained unease.

But it is at a further level of metrical variation that Harrison makes the poem's concluding and conclusive point. Whereas the father's three lines of speech at the station bookstall are appropriately irregular in their rhythm (with added syllables or abrupt shifts of stress reducing the iambic metre to no more than a faint echo before the sudden return to regularity in the last two feet), the two lines of quoted verse are perfect iambic pentameters. Harrison's reference to 'broken lines' can then be read as applying to the 'Yorkshire Dales' poems (as well, of course, as the railway lines and his father's last words) only if 'broken' is interpreted in a cultural, rather than a narrowly technical, sense. What their metrical regularity strongly suggests is a realisation on Harrison's part that an attempt to become a kind of folksy dialect poet would be to play into the hands of hegemonic form – and, hence, of bourgeois ideology – more certainly than trying to express the truth of his estrangement. Such well-groomed displays of provincial quaintness reveal how thoroughly domesticated

19

(broken-in), creatively exhausted (broken-down) and culturally displaced (broken-from-history) they are.

'Now the pentameter is a dead form and its continued use (e.g. by Philip Larkin) is in the strict sense reactionary.'[26] Writing in the early 1980s, Easthope was right about Larkin, whose outlook was obviously compatible with the ideology of bourgeois form. However, plenty of Harrison's 'School of Eloquence' sonnets were already available at that time as proof that the pentameter, and still more the iamb itself, was neither inescapably 'dead' nor 'reactionary'. In the right hands it could be remade as a powerful instrument of social struggle, a radical discourse recalling its heyday in 'the struggle for bourgeois hegemony' in the early seventeenth century.[27] But to bring off such a recuperative feat requires immense technical skill, driven by a passion for social change. Enter the grudge! Only where a radical stance on behalf of the oppressed is least in evidence is there the greatest likelihood that the pentameter will have its own way:

> And so between Big Ben and Wren's great dome
> the National Theatre has made its home.
> This (one of London's choicest) Thames-side site,
> between St Paul's and Parliament's just right.
> Somewhere between devotion and debate
> a nation's drama animates the state.
> A folly? No! No 'concrete Xanadu'
> the nation's committed its resources to.

This is part of a 'Prologue' 'intended to have been spoken by Mr Albert Finney from the Olivier stage of the National Theatre on the occasion of its inauguration'.[28] The off-the-peg doggerel of which it largely consists is a direct consequence of Harrison's attempt to marry his sincere search for a truly communal drama of ideas with the mutual backslapping of the London theatrical establishment. Perhaps Finney was too embarrassed to deliver it. In any case, it proves that Harrison's technical facility, great as it is, cannot make convincing poetry where the cutting edge of political conviction is blunted.

Sexual politics in The Loiners

> . . . human freedom is not only a private affair – but
> it is nothing at all unless it is *also* a private affair.
>
> (Herbert Marcuse)

'A private affair', yes – and an affair of the privates, if I can extend Marcuse's meaning more explicitly (and with perfectly apt crudeness) into the realm which *The Loiners* so clearly occupies. 'Loiners' is a local word, probably coined by university students, for the townspeople of Leeds; but the echo of 'loins' indicates the poems' concern with sexuality as a potential source of creative growth and, perhaps, also of conflict with the forces of repression. It is through their sexuality that the Loiners express their confused or guilt-ridden or rebellious relations with a social reality typified by inequality and the misuse of power. Even pubescent arousal does not preclude some sympathy for the animal victims of abattoirs and the human victims of Nazi death-camps:

> . . . I cried
> For the family still pent up in my balls,
> For my corned beef sandwich, and for genocide.
>
> ('Allotments', *SP*, p. 19)

If this comes close to trivialising the Holocaust, it is justified in taking the risk. Adolescent libido is so strong that to be capable of acknowledging the horror of genocide at all under such circumstances is an important advance of moral consciousness for the young boy. In fact, the life-enhancing and life-creating aspects of sexuality are offered as the very route by which Harrison arrives at some appreciation of what mass murder means. The tears that are shed in these last three lines are the product alike of sexual frustration and a dawning realisation that the pleasure principle should not deny – that it ultimately cannot *afford* to deny – knowledge of the forces that threaten life.

Published in 1970, *The Loiners* was immediately recognised as being centrally concerned with sex. One reviewer spoke of its presentation of sex as 'a fundamental test and sample of any man's attitudes to racialism, politics, conventional morality, the terror of dying'.[1] This was certainly a valuable pointer in the right direction, despite its failure to acknowledge that the poems occasionally deal with women's sexuality as well as men's. In fact, it is now possible to see how much the whole sequence owes, directly or indirectly, to the sexual and political liberationism of the 1960s as typified by the radicalised Freudianism of Wilhelm Reich, Herbert Marcuse and Norman O. Brown.

My epigraph is taken from Marcuse's *Eros and Civilization*,[2] one of the books which had an enormous impact on the politics of private desire and public revolt in the 1960s. Insistence on the political dimension of sexuality was a keynote of countercultural ideology, and one that sometimes came too readily to hand as an excuse for getting laid instead of engaging in more radical forms of action. Whatever the naive excesses of the decade, it should be noted that Marcuse himself was always enough of a Freudian to realise that localised sexual gratification at the expense of the full and free development of instinctual life could be as harmful, psychologically and socially, as the 'surplus-repression'[3] by which libido is harnessed to human exploitation under capitalism. Of course, the issue of *collective* resistance to sexual – let alone political – repression does not arise for Harrison's Loiners: each is cornered and alone within his or her sexual identity. Many are simply victims of a society that hates and fears sexuality. A few grasp something of sex's subversive potential as a counter-force to authoritarianism and violence. It is the rebels' dilemma, in particular, that I want to consider at some length; but first it is necessary to look at the victims.

The first section of the book deals with five characters, all but one of whom are placed squarely within the surroundings of wartime and postwar Leeds. The junk-dealer with a passion for books who starts the sequence is a vivid representation of the sort of impoverished existence from which death appears as a welcome release. Bent double by spine-wasting syphilis and terminally weakened by heart disease, Thomas Campey must plod his round of junk-collecting, though wind, weather and the 'dead weight' of his spoils combine to make his labour agonisingly hard. The Latin names of Campey's diseases ('tabes dorsalis', 'angina pectoris') and the list of authors he has indiscriminately collected comment ironically on his dogged but uncomprehending trek through what remains of his life. Even his idea of the earth turning 'to face the sun in March' falls sadly short of a grasp of the 'Copernican System' so grandly announced in the poem's title.

Like Dickens's equally gnarled and knotted Krook in *Bleak House*, Campey hoards words with a greedy, superstitious appetite for their cumulative physical weight and appearance, but – it is implied – with no knowledge of what they actually say. He dreams of death as an ultimate cure for his earthly afflictions – an access of 'leisure' that life has never allowed him. Harrison's Miltonic invocation of 'Ormus and of Ind' is a final, wry reminder of the unheroic seediness of Campey's Leeds-bound universe. Again like Krook, he epitomises the life-wasting impotence of those whose social subordination is not amenable to either expression or analysis. His probable illiteracy and certain ignorance have left Campey powerless in the face of a world that punishes him for his sexuality by withholding first the knowledge to avoid venereal disease and then the medicine and/or surgery to treat it.

Punishment of other sorts is meted out to other characters. Ginger's pubescent sexuality is beset by the taboos of the Catholic Church. He gains temporary 'relief' by cataloguing his sins to the priest; but the world outside the confessional is irresistibly exciting and dangerous. At night the local park is a sinister place where 'shell-shocked' paedophiles (themselves victims of an imperialist war) offer sweets to youngsters. As he runs away from them, his rote-learnt 'Aves' and 'Paternosters' are not powerful enough to mitigate his fear of damnation or to save him from his father's belt. Forgiveness and redemption are no match for Church and family as the twin institutions that police libido.

In 'The Pocket Wars of Peanuts Joe' the protagonist is caught (according to the poem's epigraph) 'right in the mangle' of working-class sexual repression, a perfect scapegoat for the community's fear of libido. His formidable cock is imaged as a rifle and an anti-aircraft gun; it can 'gush Hiroshimas'. His wanking is granted an anarchistic spontaneity in contrast to the rampant nationalism and triumphalism of VE Day. Arrested for exposing himself during the National Anthem, Joe is carted off to police cells where he ends up 'gutted like a fish/ On army issue blades', presumably by his own hand, because 'poor Penis' could not survive in a society where there are more kicks than pricks. Harrison extends the criticism of surplus repression to an attempted debunking of Natopolitan militarism in the last line-and-a-half:

> His last wish
> Bequeathed his gonads to the Pentagon.
> (*SP*, p. 17)

Unfortunately, the extravagance of this – though it is certainly funny – dissipates the force of the poem's argument. Instead of being finally opposed to militarism, Joe's cock is comically aligned with the phallic pretensions of organised male violence. This would not matter in a poem that was aiming to discredit the phallic in sex as much as in war; but that is obviously not the text's intention. We are clearly meant to sympathise with Joe, yet that sympathy is compromised – for me at least – by Joe's own non-ironic treatment of his 'weapon' as a weapon.

Another deviant figure appears in 'A Proper Caution', the poem that completes Part One (omitted from *SP*). Its title suggests equally 'a right character' and 'an apt warning'. The fat, androgynous-looking man makes his Canute-like gesture in front of 'the cuddlesome and cute' on the beach to remind them that 'death and darkness' are active forces in the world. 'Red-conked and ludicrous', like a McGill postcard archetype of comic stoicism, 'but still a man', he challenges the adequacy of the pleasure principle in the seaside heartland of working-class recreation. It is not that Harrison has suddenly changed his mind about the importance of pleasure; it is rather that he thinks libido too valuable a source of subversive energy to be contained within institutionalised forms from which nothing can be learnt and by which nothing can be challenged. 'Cuddlesomeness' and 'cuteness' are the travesties which a candyfloss culture substitutes for the sweat and semen of authentic carnality. The fat man's 'Kiss Me' hat is a perfect metonymy for the coy insipidity of publicly sanctioned sex.

The victims I have considered so far are characterised by their inability to understand their predicament or – in the case of 'A Proper Caution' – by the sheer scale of the problem they confront. In the more transparently autobiographical 'Allotments' we encounter an adolescent boy trying to experience heterosexual lovemaking in a society inimical to anything but intramarital and thoroughly repressed sexuality. It is, in fact, a world of life-denial which forces youngsters to seek sexual fulfilment near graveyards and an abattoir. The proximity of sex and death is further reinforced by the Pole who has been 'at Auschwitz and at Buchenwald', and who interrupts Harrison and his girlfriend to talk to them about the bloody business of animal slaughter and meat-eating. Later, celebrations of the end of the war offer Harrison the prospect of much greater sexual freedom:

> I felt
> Street bonfires blazing for the end of war
> VE and J burn us like lights, but saw
> Lush prairies for a tumble, wide corrals,
> A Loiner's Elysium . . .
>
> (*SP*, p. 19)

After this playing on the procreative implications of 'Loiner', the sex–death connection is made to yield the moral insight referred to in my opening paragraph. What Part One as a whole proposes is a view of the personal in which sex is both a focus of repression and an arena of potential (but mostly missed) growth and change. My epigraph from Marcuse advances the claims of the personal at the same time as it insists on the inescapability of the social. In Part Two of *The Loiners* Tony Harrison takes a step further his treatment of the complex and contradictory relationship between both these vital spheres of sexual politics. However, there is one more victim to discuss before the varieties of understanding and resistance can be properly addressed.

There is not a more original poem in this remarkable collection than 'The Nuptial Torches', which begins Part Three. It is the only poem that deals with people and events unconnected with Leeds, with England or even with the twentieth century. Its inclusion can be justified, on structural grounds, only by its overwhelming relevance to the central themes which Harrison is examining. Indeed, for the intensity of its treatment of sexuality, repression and death, it is an indispensable advance on the poems already discussed. Narrated in the first person by Isabella of Spain, it deals with the mass burning of heretics on the day of her marriage to Philip II. The girl's fascinated horror at the spectacle is caught in a series of mercilessly vivid images: flesh is 'wrung/ Bone dry'; it crumples 'like a coverlid'; it ravels up 'into /dry knots' and 'souls/ Splut through . . . pores like porridge holes'; skin 'grows/ Puckered round the knees like rumpled hose'. With dread she imagines her wedding night spoilt by memories of the victims' sufferings and, with equal dread, she anticipates 'those hateful tricks' which Philip is said to feel like after watching people burn. Philip's sexual sadism is associated so closely with fire and torture that he becomes diabolical:

> O let the King be gentle and not loom
> Like Torquemada in the torture room,
> Those wiry Spanish hairs, these nuptial nights,
> Crackling like lit tapers in his tights,
> His seed like water spluttered off hot stone
>   . . . O cure and cool
> The scorching birthmarks of his branding-tool.
>
>   (*SP*, p. 61)

Harrison offers us something much more disturbing than a pantomime demon: Philip exemplifies the death instinct as both a sexual perversion and a principle of political action. 'In a repressive civilization, death itself becomes an instrument of repression. . . . The powers that be have a deep affinity to death; death is a token of unfreedom, of defeat.'[4] Marcuse's words could serve as a useful second epigraph to the poem, for they state what the poem so effectively demonstrates: the 'deep affinity' that binds a negative inversion of the life instinct to the realities of political power. Philip's talk of God is another, deadlier, version of the prohibitions invoked against Ginger and Peanuts Joe; and, whereas 'Allotments' deals obliquely with the actual torments of murdered Jews, here we are made to face the full enormity of organised barbarism. Again, Marcuse offers a precise formulation:

'Not those who die, but those who die before they must and want to die, those who die in agony and pain, are the great indictment against civilization.'[5] To this it is necessary to add that Isabella's fate, though it comes short of death, is also an indictment of a repressive civilisation – more specifically, of patriarchal power within marriage; for her body is as much subject to the whims of tyranny as are the bodies of Carlos de Sessa and Ponce de la Fuente. Her anguished 'They curled like foetuses, *maman*, and cried' simultaneously confirms her life-affirming sensitivity and adds one more emphasis to the scandal of what awaits her. I shall return later to the implications this direct rendering of female experience has for a reading of Harrison's gender position.

In 'The White Queen', which occupies most of Part Two of the collection, Harrison introduces a deviant but defiant character whose very marginality is a source of insight. It was a major achievement of the 1960s that whole categories of the despised and rejected began to gain some sympathetic recognition, not least for the critical light which their off-centre perspective might throw on the ideological structures of 'normal' social life. As a homosexual paedophile the White Queen is undeniably beyond the pale of English legality, let alone respectability. Yet he is also a university professor (of English, needless to say) and, more importantly, a white man; so that his nickname itself can be seen as bluntly setting his sexual deviancy alongside the skin colour, education and income by which he is socially empowered in a black African country. Though the latest coup heralds a clampdown on gays, there has so far been plenty of opportunity for indulging his sexual preferences in a society where black boys can be easily and openly bought. In this respect the Queen exemplifies a long-established, but largely unacknowledged, motivation for imperialism – what one historian has called 'the export of surplus sexual energy'.[6] In the context of this poem this means that white neo-colonials can enjoy a degree of sexual freedom that would be impossible in England. But the Queen is perceptive enough to recognise the racism and sexism which infect his own 'liberated' conduct:

> I can't escape
> Our foul conditioning that makes a rape
> Seem natural, if wrong, and love unclean

Between some ill-fed blackboy and fat queen.

(*SP*, p. 22)

Healthy as this *mea culpa* is, it overlooks the fact that – racism apart – the Queen is profiting sexually from an unequal and exploitative cash relationship. Like André Gide's Immoralist, he is seeking some way of reconciling libidinous release with human responsibility; but that is a difficult task in the context of such blatant economic imperialism. He is 'bored with almost all/ The issues but the point of love', where 'the point' can be taken as both 'purpose' and 'moment'. The 'pure sex' he is looking for is similarly ambiguous: is it sex 'only' or sex 'untainted'? In either case there is no escaping the fact that it is a neocolonial ethos that allows him to express his sexuality: white desublimation feeds off black subordination. This is unequivocally recognised and owned up to in one of the dozen 'Zeg-Zeg Postcard' poems not reprinted in *Selected Poems*. Originally numbered IX, it says simply: 'What begins in honest lust can end/ with innocent blood on its hands' (*L*, p. 41). It was probably left out in order to make the White Queen less insistently insightful about his situation. But whatever may be gained by more psychological realism or less overt moralising, we are denied a sudden stab of self- and social awareness the equal of which is not to be found anywhere else in the whole *Loiners* collection.

Harrison tries hard to vindicate the White Queen. He makes a powerful bid for our sympathy in paragraph three of the poem's first section:

Things can be so much better. Once at least
A million per cent. Policeman! Priest!
You'll call it filthy, but to me it's love,
And to him it was. It *was*. O he could move
Like an oiled (slow-motion) racehorse at its peak,
Outrageous, and not gentle, tame, or meek –
O magnificently shameless in his gear,
He sauntered the flunkied restaurant, queer
As a clockwork orange and not scared.
God, I was grateful for the nights we shared.

My boredom melted like small cubes of ice
In warm sundowner whiskies. Call it vice;
Call it obscenity; it's love; so there;
Call it what you want. *I just don't care.*

                                        (*SP*, p. 22)

Here the carefully deployed echoes of Thomas Wyatt's 'They flee
from me . . . ' help to give the Queen's self-advocacy considerable
emotional weight. This is language that above all insists on
mitigating nothing and apologising for nothing. From bungled
buggery to the highbrow chatter of a literary party, the Queen
tells it all with lethal precision. At one moment he recalls a mental
breakdown in England:

                          I . . . must
        Never again be locked away or trussed
        Like a squealing piglet because my mind
        Shut out all meaning like a blackout blind.
        Next door, erotomaniacs. Here, queers,
        And butch nurses with stiff hoses mock
        As we grow limp, *Roundheads* and *Cavaliers*,
        Like King Charles bowing to the chopping block.

                                        (*SP*, p. 24)

Thus the Queen is offered as an epitome of beleaguered humanity
opposed by the sex hatred of institutional 'normality'. Compared
with this violence there is an obvious attractiveness about the
tumescent excitement of Africa:

        My white shorts tighten
        in the market crowds.
        I don't know
        if a lean Fulani boy
        or girl gave me this stand
        trailing his/her knuckles
        on my thigh.

                (*SP*, p. 35, no. II)

29

The Queen's appeal is further enhanced by his description of two fellow-whites, both victims of crippled sexuality. The first is a woman schoolteacher whose frustration finds temporary relief in alcohol. Her torments are metonymies for the larger exactions of (white) sexual and (black) political control. Over-repressed herself, she can only respond repressively to the unabashed copulating of her black servant: 'Boy!/ She'll give you the sack for those grunts of joy.' The other martyr to sex-gone-sour is a Russian doctor whose professional ministrations to the university white community ('pep- and sleeping pills') are useless against its sense of futility. Like a Graham Greene antihero, he reads Pascal on the double bed his wife has left to return to what she claims is freedom in Switzerland. He and the teacher find no escape from their predicaments, whereas the White Queen can at least regard his sexual adventures as a form of protest.

If the White Queen is equivocal about his personal stake in imperialism, there is no denying the force of attacks on imperialism elsewhere in this Part. Section 3 is a sequence of three 'travesties' (i.e. approximate translations) which all confront the irrationalities and injustices of white–black relations. The first poem, based on Hieronymus Fracastorius's treatise on syphilis, is by far the hardest-hitting. Syphilis, brought to Europe from the plundered Americas, is the central metonymy for all the cross-infections caused by territorial greed. The New World of the conquistadors will prove to be nothing more than an extension of the Old World, except that there will be a higher price to pay for the ruthless exploitation of New World people and their lands. This is a powerful antidote to the romance of imperial trade celebrated in John Masefield's 'Cargoes', a once ubiquitous school anthology poem from which Harrison takes his title 'Distant Ophir'. The next two poems (both omitted from *SP*) return to the personal, one describing a white man through the eyes of a black lover, the other a Negro dancer as seen by a white spectator. The first is especially effective in exposing how Europeans disclaim any evolutionary or cultural kinship with blacks:

> Lover, under your bleak landscape are
> rivers of strange blood, where you may see
> lily and lotus, rose and nenuphar;
> and there you'll see a restless spirit stare

and turn, your ancestor's dark shadow flee,
who gave the frizzle to your golden hair.
('The Ancestor', *L*, p. 33)

The linking of politics and disease that is so strikingly established
in 'Distant Ophir' (the syphilis poem) occurs again in Section 4
where we return to the White Queen's sexual activities. The third
and largest part of this Section, 'The Foreign Body', treats the
pathology of imperialism as a tropical disease: 'Boom! Boom! World
War 3's/ waging in my arteries.' The Queen's body becomes a body
politic that registers the invasive attacks of insects like a world beset
by national rivalries. A rain-sodden atlas images the futility of both
British imperialism and the Queen's antics:

That Empire flush diluted is
pink as a lover's orifice,
then *Physical*, *Political* run
first into marblings and then one
mud colour, the dirty, grey,
flat reaches of infinity.

The one red thing, I squat and grab
at myself like a one-clawed crab.
(*SP*, p. 34)

The Queen's whiteness has given way to a 'redness' that suggests
resolute opposition to the forces of sexual-political repression.
Yet we are reminded of Prufrock's 'pair of ragged claws' and
the longed-for oblivion they represent. Here the crab is only
one-clawed, and its grabbing is a desperate attempt at personal
survival via masturbatory self-absorption. To be sure, there is
nothing intrinsically wrong with masturbation, but redness carries a
political implication from which the Queen clearly shrinks in favour
of sex as a refuge. His own body politic remains a site of passive
infection (and partial collusion), rather than an instrument of active
resistance. My epigraph from Marcuse stresses the importance of
the private, but only as one element (albeit indispensable) in a
total emancipatory project. Harrison's White Queen suffers the

self-defeating contradictions that attend a failure to relate private resentment to an adequate politics of public liberation.

The last two poems in Part Two are thoroughly ambivalent treatments of white male colonial sexual attitudes. Their protagonist is a sixty-year-old Public Works Department employee in Nigeria. He cheerfully tells of his exploits with young native girls in rhymed lines that vary from twelve to fifteen syllables. Each leisurely five- to six-stress line helps to establish the conversational ease and confessional frankness of the PWD Man's idiom. The substance of his attitude to black people can be found in the following passage:

> Though I'm not your socialistic, go-native-ite type chap
> With his flapping, nig-nog dresses and his dose of clap,
> I have my finer feelings and I'd like to make it clear
> I'm not just itchy fingers and a senile lecher's leer.
> I have my qualms of conscience and shower *silver*, if you
> please,
> To their lepers and blind beggars kipping under trees.
> They're agile enough, those cripples, scrabbling for the
> coins,
> But not half so bloody agile as those furry little groins
> I grope for through strange garments smelling of dye-pits
> As I graze my grizzly whiskers on those black, blancmangy
> tits.
> I don't do bad for sixty.
>
> (*SP*, p. 42)

There should be no mistaking the complacent hypocrisy of this: the man is despicable in his attempt to justify his exploitation of black girls' bodies. Yet he is also an exponent of the philosophy summed up in the first poem's epigraph from Andrei Voznesensky: 'We were not born to survive, alas,/ But to step on the gas.' His inveterate randiness is contrasted favourably with state-supported enfeeblement: 'Yes, better to put the foot down, go fast, accelerate,/ Than survive on your arses, mope and squawk and wait/ For Death to drop the darkness over twittering age/ Like a bit of old blanket on a parrot's cage.' His Yorkshire childhood is invoked at the end of the first poem to validate the clear-eyed courage with which he refuses to accept defeat. Above all, he wants to be remembered for 'the hole he's made', even if, like the goat in the second poem's Abakua epigraph, he must pay with his own skin for breaking the drum.

In the second poem the PWD Man is on his way back to Leeds. His musings about retirement, with no black girls and nothing but his fist to fuck, are punctuated by a refrain that recalls in one of its lines the White Queen's politically compromised sexuality: 'My body's like a blow-up globe all blotched with Empire red.' However, the context constructs a tough old-stager determined to go out with a bang. Imperialism is cosmeticised as 'Atlasitis, Atlasitis, British Isles Disease', as though the scale and rapacity of Britain's territorial expansionism could be attributed simply to an inveterate national urge to see the world. Even if a heavy emphasis on imperialism-as-disease is conceded, there is no escaping a proportionate emphasis on that disease as a heroic cross which the PWD Man and his country have to bear. In that respect at least, it is a view almost indistinguishable from Kipling's.

Sex as a means of cross-cultural communication is shifted from the British Empire to the Iron Curtain in a series of poems in Part Three. 'The Curtain Catullus', 'The Bedbug' and 'The Chopin Express' all treat sex as a subversive activity which denies frontiers and challenges state repression. Cold War regimentation is opposed by the honest compulsions of the pleasure principle: 'No cause or class/ Can take the pleasure from between your hips.' It is as seductive an idea as that of Peanuts Joe brandishing his prick as an antidote to nationalistic prejudice. Unfortunately, it is just as politically naive; for, as Orwell's Winston Smith realised, it takes more than a fuck to resist repression. Simulating love-moans for a bedroom bugging device ('The Bedbug') does not go any way towards making a world where such obscene surveillance is not practised. Celebrating copulation as a *lingua franca* of international solidarity ('Brave cocks and cunts/ belong to no barbed continents') appears to deny the relevance of non-sexual politics; but the poems cannot avoid acknowledging that much more than sex is involved in an apparently 'neutral' sexual encounter:

I felt the broken world all come
together then, and all between

a conshie and a commie bum.
('The Chopin Express', *L*, p. 70)

It is enormously significant that the man is a 'conshie', though
the text does not foreground the point. His reason for being
in an Eastern Bloc country is thus revealed as a principled
opposition to the Vietnam War, not merely the globe-trotting of
a bohemian pleasure-seeker. Harrison's attempted endorsement
of a one-dimensional Marcuseanism is effectively deconstructed
by his intimation of the wider political universe of which Marcuse
himself was only too well aware. Indeed, the 'empire we can't
get away from' is more adequately recognised in 'The Excursion'
(omitted from *SP*), a poem dedicated to Harrison's 'friends in
Prague' but taking Hexham Cathedral in Northumberland as
the focus of its observations on the historical and geographical
continuities of imperialism:

> A slot marked *Biafra*
> in the south aisle wall
> replaces *Destitute Clergy*
> or *Sunday School*.
> I feed it the four
> bob I remember a European paid,
> plus a tin of indigenous corned beef,
> to two dumpy Ibo whores
> for pulling him off
> in a matter of seconds,
> scared stiff of syphilis,
> nothing half so civil
> as miscegenation.
>
> (*L*, pp. 71–2)

Four bob for the starving and four bob for a hand-job. It is as
though the one is a gesture of balance and atonement for the other;
but the arithmetic is wrong. Western imperialism is always ready
to spend more in exploiting the Third World than in helping it, so
the whores get the bonus of corned beef while the text slides into

uncritical approval of miscegenation as such. Would fucking the whores really have been more 'civil' than being wanked by them? The ideology of sex as a subversive anti-politics says yes; other currents throughout *The Loiners* show that miscegenation is entirely compatible with – even necessary to – the smooth functioning of neocolonial oppression.

It is to Harrison's gender-position that we must look for an explanation of his readiness to accept sexual release as a substitute for political emancipation. For what invariably redeems Harrison's protagonists is a male mythology of resolute personal authenticity in the face of ageing and the intrusiveness – in one form or another – of society. Only in 'The Nuptial Torches' are we offered a sensitive rendering of a woman's experience, and it is surely significant that only there do we get an unequivocal endorsement of the claims of humanity over those of genitality. At the time when Harrison was writing the poems in this collection – during the 1960s – the idea of liberation by libido ('Make love, not war!') was everywhere prevalent. What had barely begun to be examined was how far such rampant genitality was a self-serving masculine mystique which would not, by itself, further either women's interests or those of oppressed people generally. Harrison perfectly articulates the ideological confusion of this cultural moment: *The Loiners* stands at a vital point of transition between the Swinging Sixties and the feminist seventies. Nowhere is its representative ambivalence more strikingly obvious than in the two poems that complete the whole sequence as Parts Four and Five.

'Newcastle is Peru' begins – like Robert Lowell's 'Waking Early Sunday Morning', an obvious formal and thematic influence[7] – with a domestic scene that is immediately situated in a world context of war and death. Harrison's drunken efforts to light a fire with a Sunday newspaper bring home in every sense the realities of the global village in which the personal and the public, the past and present, the remote and intimate are linked together. The newspaper headlines and 'nine or ten *Newcastle Brown*' combine to set Harrison's mind racing wildly around memorable episodes from his past. He remembers his childhood excitement at fairgrounds where being spun round in a 'Chair-o-plane' gave to those in orbit the illusion of free-floating liberation. He remembers the Leeds flat he shared with his wife, and his time in Prague.

Finally, he returns to Newcastle and its imaginary transformation into Peru.

There are glimpses of Tyneside and the Andes, each partially merged with the other, and these give way to an attempted affirmation of 'the gravity of love' which offers a metaphor for universal harmony. However, with the recognition 'that we brave/ harsh opposition when we love', the argument shifts to one of insisting on the vulnerability of romantic love to 'the world's bold cannonade/ Of loveless warfare and cold trade'. Peru now becomes, not a distant land of rich pickings for imperialistic plunder, but the body of Harrison's wife. Yet even the rapt exploration of her body cannot keep at bay recognition of the wider world of our own and other people's experience. Love cannot set boundaries to our interaction with the unknown:

> My fingerprints still lined with coal
> send cold shudders through my soul.
> Each whorl, my love-, my long life-line,
> mine, inalienably mine,
> lead off my body as they press
> onwards into nothingness.
> I see my grimy fingers smudge
> everything they feel or touch.
>
> (*SP*, p. 67)

This is an impasse of which Harrison has since made much more creative use in *v*. (see Chapter 5 below): the private is no final refuge from the public; but here the inescapably public dimension of the private is seen as a 'smudging' in which neither public nor private is enhanced. Harrison is left looking at a colour supplement photograph of 'aggressively fine bosoms' which mimic *'négritude'* with their expensively acquired suntan, and are displayed not for sexual arousal but as an aid to self-examination for breast cancer. In other words, what might have been a celebratory image of female eroticism turns out to be a sobering reminder of malignant growths and possible mastectomies. How sharply is Harrison's gender position thus revealed! For whose interest does the photograph serve but that of women themselves – white, middle-class, *Observer*-reading women, to be sure, but women all the same? And whose disappointment but a man's could possibly represent such a photograph as an unwelcome instance of how the world violates our privacy?

Returning to the geographical/topographical trope by which the wife's body becomes Peru, one can now identify the same masculine perspective that enabled John Donne to call his mistress 'my America! my new-found-land'[8] without, of course, questioning his right to exploit either the woman or the continent. For Harrison the woman's body functions as an object of his gaze and as a terrain for his appropriation. There is no question of her mind providing any solace or support, either as a refuge *from* the world or as an equal partner in learning to be active *in* the world. As with the White Queen's use of black boys, there is a largely unexamined distinction between sexuality as an assertion of recalcitrant individuality and genitality as an acquiescence in – and instrument of – social oppression. The image of fingers begriming everything they touch offers a starting point for a critique of male egoism, but the chance is not taken. Again, in the last stanza, there is the image of the fire 'strutting' upon the bed as if to focus the arrogance with which Harrison has enticed the woman into it; but once again the imaginative grasp exceeds the ideological understanding, and the narcissistic self-display of the firelight is promptly transferred to the 'aggressively fine bosoms' which so confuse Harrison's complacent masculinity.[9]

Robert Lowell's final image of life-sapping circularity in 'Waking Early Sunday Morning', 'our monotonous sublime', does nothing to mitigate the horror of American or global public life. At the same time the poem refuses to side with a romantic notion of heroic personal resistance: its 'anywhere, but somewhere else!' is a reminder of the futility of that urge for withdrawal from the political which Harrison's position partially endorses. To be sure, there are several images of circularity and repetition in 'Newcastle is Peru' which seem to insist that the gravitational pull of the public should not be mistaken for free-floating individuality; and the 'gravity of love' as an ideal of universal harmony is identified as a desperate illusion alongside the 'harsh opposition' which romantic love must actually face. However, the romance of the private gets a new lease of life as an embattled, masculine selfhood that can find fulfilment neither in an active engagement with the public, political world nor in a more complete personal relationship than one of sexual enticement and conquest.

'Ghosts: Some Words Before Breakfast' puts Harrison's sexual attitudes to a final, fascinating test. It deals with the difficult birth of a baby girl from the perspective of the father as he helplessly watches his wife's suffering and his daughter's struggle for life. Confronted with his daughter's physical frailty, Harrison is torn between willing her to live and wishing her free from 'a lifetime's crippledom'. He realises his inability to relieve her pain or prevent her death, if die she must: ' . . . my kiss can't make you less/the helpless prey of Nothingness'. Yet his medically ineffectual kiss is represented as a humanly nourishing gesture which can unite several generations:

> Mother, all, *all*, of us in this
> brave trophallaxis of a kiss
> that short-circuits generations scent
> mortality's rich nutriment.
> (*SP*, p. 73)

The superbly ambiguous last line holds in balance the life-enhancing power of love and the way love, in turn, is fuelled by the realisation of how short and vulnerable life is. Harrison's mother is addressed at this point because she had regarded an earlier stillborn child, conceived before marriage, as 'just/ retribution for our filthy lust'. Working-class puritanism is challenged by the assertion that love must be spontaneous and generous, that it is the measure of how fully we live our lives, since none of us can escape the consequences of our mortality: 'Love's not something you can hoard/ against the geriatric ward.' A bold statement of sixties sexual liberationism if ever there was one, neatly eliding love and libido as it does.

In an agony of powerlessness Harrison leafs through the sci-fi super-hero comics in the 'airless' hospital waiting-room. He imagines the 'male silhouette' on the street-crossing signs which 'still strides/ off the caution and just keeps/ on striding . . . / into his element, the dark', an image of questing humanity and mortality that will resonate subversively at the end of the poem. The lorry-drivers on the Great North Road with their cargoes of 'Newcastle Brown' plunge Harrison into a series of nightmare images related to his daughter's plight. He comes back to reality with an extended description of the Tyne ferry, the river itself and the sea, culminating in a direct comparison of his daughter's physical survival with his own survival as a writer:

> Blood transfusion, saline drip,
> 'this fiddle' and 'stiff upper lip'
> have seen us so far.
> You'll live
> like your father, a contemplative.
> (*SP*, p. 75)

He has been sustained by poetry ('this fiddle', in Marianne Moore's famous phrase) and by his English masculine stoicism. These have been the equivalents of his daughter's life-support system.

The best future Harrison can envisage for his daughter is that she should grow up to be as self-sufficiently introspective as he is himself. That self-sufficiency, however, is put in doubt by the poem's conclusion:

> Mother, wife and daughter, ghost –
> I've laid, laid, laid, laid
> you, but I'm still afraid,
> though now Newcastle's washed with light
> about the next descent of night.
> (*SP*, p. 76)

It is a complex set of ghosts which Harrison has invoked and only partially put to rest. As in Ibsen's play, there is a transgenerational legacy of sexual 'disease' (his mother's life-denying puritanism); but there are also the ghostly images of his own powerlessness conjured up by the sci-fi comics and the beer tankers. Finally, there is the nightmare prospect of Jane's (the daughter's) death, or her surviving as a helpless cripple. And all these 'ghosts' have been raised in the first place because Harrison has 'laid' his wife. Thus, though I do not think the text intends it, we are left with a troubled and troubling statement of Harrison's beleaguered masculinity, even as he tries to hold on to an optimistic idea of his daughter's following in his footsteps. The fear to which the text freely confesses is that his wife and/or daughter will be permanently damaged or die – that his mother's retributive obsession will thus have the last word – but beneath that is the fear that 'the next descent of night' will bring with it the spectre of insufficiency that haunts a view of women as mere incarnations of male guilt (mother), male libido (wife) and male pride (daughter). The confident male striding into 'his element, the dark' is an image not just of questing humanity but also of a son, husband and father for whom being 'a contemplative' holds as much threat as promise.

It is entirely characteristic of Harrison's gender position that in 'Ghosts' he should look for self-definition to super-hero comics, the male silhouette and beer-tanker drivers. Where women appear at all in *The Loiners* it is usually as the objects of men's gaze and the targets of their libido. In fact, we are rarely offered whole women, only the bits of them that are required for male arousal:

> Everything in this rich dark
> craves my exclamation mark.
> Wife! Mouth! Breasts! Thigh!

and

> our flesh
> gleaming: breasts; thigh; bum;
> ('The Heart of Darkness', *SP*, p. 39)

Once again, the exception to this is 'The Nuptial Torches', a poem that gains in stature and significance the more it is compared with other poems in the collection. Only here is a woman treated as a moral subject whose feelings form the bedrock of compassion on which the text's meaning is centred. Isabella's is the authentic voice of the sexually exploited. As such, it has the authority to speak for the other victims in the poem. Nowhere else in the collection are women allowed their own voice to speak for themselves or anyone else.

40

The Loiners explores sexuality with a frankness and concentrated attention that are astonishing. The whole sequence is a major achievement of structural coherence and compelling local detail. If I have concentrated on places where that structure and those details are under pressure from largely unexamined ideological assumptions, that is only to emphasise the enormous significance of the collection for anyone who wishes to understand the full scope – and ultimate limits – of sexual politics in the 1960s. Harrison's next collections go on to examine issues of class and language with, on the whole, a finer sense of how the public and the personal interact. Nevertheless, in all the variety and depth of Harrison's later work there is no greater challenge to a properly cultural criticism than *The Loiners*.

FOOTNOTE ON 'CURTAIN SONNETS'

A group of five fourteen-line 'Curtain Sonnets', originally published in the 'other poems' section of From *'The School of Eloquence' and other poems*, is added to the *Loiners* sequence in *Selected Poems* (pp. 55–9). They do not entirely compensate for the loss of twelve 'Zeg-Zeg Postcard' poems, 'The Excursion', 'The Chopin Express' and two of the original three 'Travesties'. However, they offer useful snapshots of some of the attitudes discussed above. 'Guava Libre' is a defiant display of ludic ingenuity in finding how many sexual metaphors (all female) can be applied to a bottle of guavas given to Harrison by the film actress Jane Fonda. They met in Leningrad, where both were working (he as lyricist) on George Cukor's film *The Blue Bird*. That city is the focus of the next three sonnets, its cold joylessness challenged by sporadic outbursts of subversive pleasure. But best of the five is the last sonnet, set in Prague on Harrison's birthday. (We are not told which, but he was in Prague in 1967, and that seems the most probable time.) It centres on a gargoyle whose wide-mouthed fixity of expression prompts speculation about its relationship to the 'cherries' and 'blow-ups of Karl Marx' down below in the streets. Though May will begin the very next day, there is an air of political and emotional petrifaction about the city. It has been frozen for a long time, like the gargoyle whom 'Medusa must have hexed . . . in mid-song' (an early encounter with 'the gaze of the Gorgon'). Nevertheless, the thaw ('late' and 'slow') is on its way, as melted snow dribbles down the gargoyle's chin.

There is a fine balance of positive and negative implications in this image: if there is to be a release from repression at last, will it be drooled away in mindless self-indulgence or otherwise wasted on a people too long denied the experience of genuine artistic and emotional freedom? The 'Prague Spring' of 1968 was one of the high points of the freedom struggle in the 1960s. This poem registers the hungover, depressive aftermath of those heady days, even as it (apparently) anticipates them. It offers a retrospective starting point for the sort of comradely critique of sixties liberationism I have attempted in this chapter.

3

Translations, adaptations
and theatre work

How long
Do works endure? As long
As they are not completed.
Since as long as they demand effort
They do not decay.
(Bertolt Brecht, 'About the Way to
Construct Enduring Works')

'If he were a modern writer, Palladas would not be considered a nice man' (*Astley*, p. 136). Peter Levi's assessment of the fourth century poet suggests something of his appeal for Tony Harrison. Harrison himself has been similarly unequivocal about the man: 'He is one of those embarrassing but heroic figures who are not dignified in despair, refusing to be noble on the gallows or to make peace with their maker' (*P*, p. 9). The 'nihilistic scorn' (*P*, p. 10) with which Palladas surveyed the terminal decline of paganism in the face of the onslaught of militant Christianity has a great deal in common with the White Queen's view of colonial Africa sixteen hundred years later; and it is thus in a direct line of development from much of the tone and content of *The Loiners*. However, there is also an anticipation of the mordant savagery of *U.S. Martial* (1981), written six years after the Palladas poems were published. The choice of two such unregenerate cynics for his only two books of non-theatrical verse translations[1] is evidence enough of Harrison's fascination with the power of pure negativity.

Behind the masks of his adopted personae, Harrison can give free rein to the sort of sentiments that would be utterly inconsistent with the dominant radicalism and compassion of the 'School of Eloquence' sonnets or the balancing of positive and negative forces

43

attempted in 'A Kumquat for John Keats', which was published in the same year as *U.S. Martial*. Even the foul-mouthed skinhead in *v*. voices a critique of social injustice the scorching anger of which is a long way from the triple-distilled *Weltschmerz* of Palladas and Martial. Just how reactionary that *Weltschmerz* is can be seen in the attitudes both display towards women. Whatever insults are hurled at hypocrites, the wealthy, or professional shysters of every stamp, an especially fierce and sustained attention is reserved for women. In the *Palladas* sequence, there is first the henpecked stoicism of the stand-up comic:

> Poor devil that I am, being so attacked
> by wrath in fiction, wrath in fact.
>
> Victim of wrath in literature and life:
>
> 1. The *Iliad* and 2. the wife!
>
> (no. 29)

With the next poem about women, this changes into an altogether bleaker humour:

> women all
> cause rue
>
> but can be nice
> on occasional
>
> moments two
> to be precise
>
> in bed
> & dead
>
> (no. 51)

The next five poems show women as adulterous and hypocritical (no. 52), nagging and generally bothersome to men (nos. 53 and 54), insulting (no. 55) and ugly (no. 56). By number 61 the henpecked husband has become a much more thoroughgoing victim; the best that *might* be said for his predicament is that his wife is 'chaste and not *too* hard on you'. The Spartan mother of number 69 stabs her son for running away from the war and for compromising her honour by not getting killed. The only woman about whom Palladas speaks with anything but dislike is Hypatia, the Hellenistic teacher who was butchered by a Christian mob.

In *U.S. Martial*, out of a total of eighteen poems, most very short, seven are about women, and all of those depict women as the exponents *par excellence* of a Roman decadence updated to modern New York. (*USM* no. XVIII, 'Oh, Moon of Mahagonny', is discussed as an 'American poem' in Chapter 6 below.) Predatory and insatiable, Martial's women always put their sexual needs before anything else. In 'The Joys of Separation' (*USM*, no. XVI) the woman's relentless promiscuity is ignored by her husband, who is more interested in fictional adultery:

> *She* wants more and more and more new men in her.
>
> *He* finally finishes *Anna Karenina*.

That the husband is able to finish *Anna Karenina* hints at the scale of the wife's sexual appetite. Poem XVII, 'Sandwich Bawd Swing Song', turns the troilism of the sexual 'sandwich' into a metaphor for America getting metaphorically fucked between Soviet Communism abroad and Black Power at home. Number XI deals with lesbianism, Numbers VII and XV deal with feminine vanity and Number V offers a particularly nasty display of objectifying misogyny:

> Screw old women? Sure I do! But YOU
> you're one step further on, more corpse, than crone
> and necrophilia I'm not into!
>
> Hecuba, Niobe, both of them I'd screw
> till one became a bitch, the other stone.

Horrible as this saloon-bar cynicism is, it is thoroughly endorsed by the attitudes ascribed to women elsewhere in the sequence. Like

America itself, they deserve to be abused and degraded because they have asked for it.

The depiction of women is one of several major themes which link the translations/adaptations of Palladas and Martial to the rest of Harrison's output, including his plays and libretti. As Harrison himself has pointed out: 'Poetry is all I write, whether for books, or readings, or for the National Theatre, or for the opera house and concert hall, or even for TV' (*Astley*, p. 9). This implies a very close connection – not to say continuity – between all areas of Harrison's verse-writing. The special conditions of translation from a number of ancient, medieval and modern languages, as well as of collaboration with actors, directors and composers,[2] which apply to the dramatic verse require a more specialised study than is possible here. Nevertheless, the theatre works, written and performed from the early days of Harrison's career onwards, represent a major point of reference for contextualising and examining the poems with which this book is primarily concerned. As I have already indicated, the theme of gender is central. I shall also pay close attention to related issues of class and cultural hegemony in the discussion that follows; and I shall make detailed comments on formal and stylistic features of some of the major theatre pieces.

In the first (1973) and shorter of two prefaces to his version of Molière's *The Misanthrope*, Harrison comments:

> I have made use of a couplet similar to the one I used in *The Loiners*, running the lines over, breaking up sentences, sometimes using the odd half-rhyme to subdue the chime, playing off the generally colloquial tone and syntax against the formal structure, letting the occasional couplet leap out as an epigram in moments of devastation or wit. My floating 's is a way of linking the couplet at the joint and speeding up the pace by making the speaker deliver it as almost one line not two.[3]

This points with characteristic precision to some of the principal ways in which Harrison adapted the couplet of his early verse for transposing Molière's social satire of 1666 to a Parisian setting three hundred years later. His handling of the couplet was given another daunting challenge – this time in the direction of controlled tragic intensity – in his next theatre piece, a version of Racine's *Phèdre* set in nineteenth-century British India and called *Phaedra Britannica*. After this the couplet continued as the basic unit through a series of musical dramas, nearly all in verse, like *The Big H.* and *Medea: A Sex-War Opera*. Among his major theatre works, only *The Oresteia* has been largely without rhymed verse, and in his most recent plays the couplet still predominates, though blank verse, prose and a variety of alternative rhyme-schemes are also present.

The astonishing range of Harrison's dramatic verse, rhymed and unrhymed, can be gauged by a comparison of his translations with those of other translators. For example, Richard Wilbur's widely admired 1954 rendering of *Le Misanthrope* has Eliante comment thus on Alceste's refusal to flatter Célimène:

> Love, as a rule, affects men otherwise,
> And lovers rarely love to criticize.
> They see their lady as a charming blur,
> And find all things commendable in her.
> If she has any blemish, fault, or shame,
> They will redeem it by a pleasing name.
> The pale-faced lady's lily-white, perforce;
> The swarthy one's a sweet brunette, of course;
> The spindly lady has a slender grace;
> The fat one has a most majestic pace;
> The plain one, with her dress in disarray,
> They classify as *beauté négligée*;
> The hulking one's a goddess in their eyes,
> The dwarf, a concentrate of Paradise;
> The haughty lady has a noble mind;
> The mean one's witty, and the dull one's kind;
> The chatterbox has liveliness and verve,
> The mute one has a virtuous reserve.
> So lovers manage, in their passion's cause,
> To love their ladies even for their flaws.[4]

The Harrison version of the same speech is:

> How does that bit in old Lucretius go,
> that bit on blinkered lovers? O, you know;

47

it's something like: 'whatever's negative's
soon metamorphosed by new adjectives:
the girl whose face is pinched and deathly white
's not plain anaemic, she's "pre-Raphaelite".
The loved one's figure's like Venus de Milo's –
even the girl who weighs a hundred kilos!
"Earth Mother"'s how some doting lover dubs
his monstrous mistress with enormous bubs.
"A touch of tarbrush?" No, that's healthy tan.
The one called "Junoesque"'s more like a man.
The slut's "Bohemian", the dwarf's virtue
's *multum in parvo* like a good haiku.
There's "self respect" for arrogant conceit.
The windbag's extrovert, the dumb's "discreet";
stupidity's "good nature", slyness "wit",
et cetera . . . it's not inapposite!
(TM, p. 25; DV and TW, p. 30)

The point that should be made is not that Harrison's version is better than Wilbur's. As a matter of fact, the Wilbur version, anchored firmly in Molière's seventeenth century, is closer to the original in its rhythmic regularity and unhurried accumulation of witty instances. What makes the Harrison so good is that it manages to convey the full linguistic range – from slick demotic to highfalutin cultural references – of a 1960s Parisian intellectual socialite, without blunting any of Molière's comic cutting edge. The ingenuity of the rhyming is not a gratuitous display of virtuosity: it is a perfect vehicle for Eliante's carefully cultivated salon glitter.

In a totally different moral and emotional register is the language of Aeschylus' *Oresteia*. From the third play of the trilogy, the *Eumenides*, I take a speech by the Ghost of Clytemnestra translated by Philip Vellacott for the Penguin Classics edition of 1956. The Ghost is trying to bludgeon the Furies into a fiercer pursuit of Orestes:

In dreams you hunt your prey, baying like hounds whose
thought
Will never rest; but what of deeds? Has weariness
Conquered and softened you with sleep, till you forget

My pain? Rise up, torment his heart with just reproach;
For whetted words goad the quick conscience. Storm at
him
With hot blood-reeking blasts blown from your vaporous
womb,
Wither his hope of respite, hunt him to death![5]

For the New American Library edition (1962), Paul Roche translates
this as:

Yelping after game like silly dogs in sleep
which never can stop thinking they are on the chase.
What are you *doing*? Get up and don't give in to toil
or let yourselves go soft with sleep and leave me in my
pain.
Whip up your livers with the lashes they deserve.
For people in the right, reproaches can be spurs.
Oh, breathe upon him with that butchery breath of yours.
Shrivel him to ash from your smoking burning bowels.
Off at him again. Pursue him to the bone.[6]

Harrison's version is:

Dreaming of hunting, like dogs, but not doing!
Baying like bloodhounds that track in their slumbers.
Dreaming not *doing*! Get up and get going.
Sleep only blunts your rage at my bloodwrong.
My bloodgrudge should boost you back into action.
Bloodgrudge is a goad to upholders of bloodright.
Let your breath billow round him its gore-reeking gases.
Shrivel his flesh with hot blasts from your bowels,
fart fire through your flues till he flops like a fruitrind.
Hound him and hunt him till he sags like a skin-bag.
(*DV* and *TW*, p. 267)

This speech is Clytemnestra's last, and Aeschylus obviously intended
it to be a bloodcurdling one. I am not qualified to comment on

the semantic or stylistic fidelity of any of the above versions, but Harrison's looks as though it should be theatrically more effective than the other two. To begin with, Harrison has put his knowledge of old languages to good use by adopting the rhythmic pattern of Anglo-Saxon poetry, where lines usually fall into two balanced halves and each half is held together by alliteration – for example: 'Dreaming not *doing*! ‖ Get up and get going.'; 'Hound him and hunt him ‖ till he sags like a skin-bag.' Harrison does not often follow the Anglo-Saxon practice of alliterating across the caesura; but the pairing of words in each half-line greatly augments the cumulative rhythm of this particular speech. Its insistent beat is intensified by the accumulation of end-stopped lines, so that the final effect is one of relentless verbal hammering or drumming. Anglo-Saxon poetry also provides the model for the many compound nouns by which Harrison approximates the condensed epithets of Aeschylus. Their use establishes, more forcefully than Roche or Vellacott, the clan-based culture for which the blood feud was so powerful an institution. 'Bloodwrong . . . bloodgrudge . . . blood-right': each is as weighty with condensed cultural meaning as the 'gift-hall' and 'swan's-road' of *Beowulf*. This recuperation of Anglo-Saxon economy and strength is of a piece with Harrison's frequent recourse to Yorkshire working-class bluntness, as in Clytemnestra's comments on the dead Agamemnon and Cassandra:

> Look at him, Shaggermemnon, shameless, shaft-happy,
> ogler and grinder of Troy's golden girlhood.
> Look at her, spearprize, prophetess, princess,
> whore of his wartent, his bash back on shipboard.
>
> (*DV & TW*, p. 225)

There is no other translator with both the scholarly confidence and the sheer linguistic chutzpah to produce that 'Shaggermemnon' at such an emotionally charged moment.

Near the end of his preface to *Phaedra Britannica* (1975), Harrison writes:

> Couplets keep the cat on the hot tin roof. Each spirit has its own custom-built treadmill. After the metronome, the comic pace-maker of the *Misanthrope* couplet, I wanted a

more organic model for my iambics. I wanted to return the
iamb back to its sources in breath and blood.

(*Astley*, p. 191)

This shows the unbuttoned accessibility which characterises all
Harrison's comments on technical matters. What precedes it is an
erudite and absorbing discussion of such things as earlier treatments
of the Phaedra story, the culture of British imperialism and the
conflict between repressive rationalism and transgressive 'nature'
in Theseus/the Governor and Phèdre/the Memsahib. Nothing else
that Harrison has written or said demonstrates better that he is the
most interesting of commentators on his own work. He can quarry
a series of brilliant observations from close scrutiny of a huge range
of material, in this case from Euripides and Seneca to histories of the
Raj and the superbly titled *Terrestrial Hymns and Carnal Ejaculations*
(1682) of Alexander Radcliffe.

What emerges most consistently from the prefaces and interviews,
as well as the plays themselves, is Harrison's abiding fascination
with language and languages. Some of his most innovative theatre
pieces have been inspired by linguistic rather than literary models:
shepherds' ways of counting sheep give a choric backbone to *Yan
Tan Tethera* (1983); British, American and Scandinavian versions
of the ballad 'The Two Sisters', both spoken and acted out, form
the basis of *Bow Down* (1977); and *The Big H.*, a television piece
from 1984, is built around the vocabulary and rhythms of the
school classroom and a dizzying set of variations on the missing
or misplaced aspirate of Northern working-class speech.

In both *Bow Down* and *Medea: A Sex-War Opera* Harrison proved
that he could combine different versions of the same story in a single
dramatic work. A much bigger feat of integration was required
for his version of *The Mysteries*, begun with *The Passion* in 1977
and first performed in its three-part entirety in 1985. The four
major cycles of English medieval pageant plays – York, Wakefield,
Chester and Coventry – had to be edited, adapted and assimilated
to each other in varying degrees to produce a coherent modern
version of the traditional mystery narrative from the Creation to
the Last Judgement. Although a number of people helped in this
process – three of whom are named in a prefatory note to *The
Mysteries* (1985) – it was Harrison who was responsible for the
shape and content of the finished piece; it is his name alone that

appears on the cover of the published text. With regard to any text it is important to establish authorial responsibility, but it is especially so in a case like this, where the achievement is so enormous in terms of scholarship and stagecraft as much as linguistic skill.

The nature and scale of Harrison's labours may be judged from a few examples. The 'Last Supper' and 'Pilate and Percula' scenes (*M*, pp. 100–7) have been largely quarried from three of the York pageants (nos. 26, 27 and 30) which occupy a total of twenty-nine pages in one recent edition of the cycle.[7] Long, repetitive exchanges are cut to a few lines; lines are shifted from one scene to another and from one character to another in order to speed up the narrative development and remove the sort of minor roles that would have given a chance to perform to many of the original guild members, but would suffocate the action on a modern stage. Elsewhere whole pageants are omitted for the same reasons of economy and pace: there is no treatment of Moses and Pharaoh, the Temptation, the Transfiguration or any of the miracles except – very briefly – the healing of the blind man in 'The Entry to Jerusalem' (*M*, pp. 96–7) and the restoration of the soldier's ear in 'The Agony in the Garden' (*M*, p. 111). Harrison ignores the York pageants on the Death, Assumption and Coronation of the Virgin (nos. 44, 45, 46): in any case, these were rarely performed in the later years of the cycle's life because of their obvious Catholic resonances. Similarly, he takes little from the turgidly moralising language of the Chester cycle, and even passes over three plays by the boldly inventive Wakefield Master.

Whatever the constraints of economy, Harrison makes full use of the Wakefield Master's three best efforts, 'The Killing of Abel', 'Noah and his Sons' and, above all, the delightful 'Second Shepherds' Play';[8] but even here there is drastic pruning and one or two additions from other cycles. The pruning includes the excision of Cain's son, Pickharness, and all of Noah's family except his Wife. The 750-odd lines of the 'Second Shepherds' Play' are reduced by two-thirds without much loss of comic stage business and with a huge gain in headlong gusto. Where the language of the original is vivid and/or reasonably accessible to a modern audience, Harrison usually leaves it alone, except sometimes to edit and condense it. With the sullen crudities of Cain's first speech to Abel he lets the words of the Wakefield Master do their work without interference:

Come kiss mine arse! I will not ban:
But away from here is your welcome.
Thou should ha' stayed till thou were called,
Come near and either drive or hold,
And kiss the devil's bum.
Go graze thy sheep, under and out,
For that to thee is lief.

(*M*, pp. 25–6)

Another example of this lightness of touch is the 'Entry to Jerusalem' section, where seventy lines from York pageant 25 are left almost unaltered in their dignified simplicity. In a few instances Harrison cannot resist outdoing an already effective original, as in his version of Judas's first speech. Pageant 26 in the York text has splendid alliterative lines like 'But for the poore, ne thare parte priked me no peyne–/ But me tened for the tente parte, the trewthe to beholde,/ That thirty pens of iij hundereth so tyte I shulde tyne' (ll. 144–6). Harrison gives this a stronger metrical thrust and a Yorkshire inflection that a modern audience can quickly recognise:

The poor's plight pricked me not, to play no pretence.
What pricked me and pined me was t'loss of my pence.

(*M*, p. 100)

Four earlier lines in the York version of the same speech deal with Judas's resentment at the money spent on ointment for Jesus's feet:

Tille hym ther brought one a boyste my bale for to brewe
    That baynly to his bare feete to bowe was full braythe,
Sho anoynte tham with an oynement that nobill was and
                                                        newe,
    But for that werke that sche wrought I wexe woundir
                                                        wrothe.
(ll. 131–4)

Harrison shifts the anointing to Jesus's hair in a rendering that gives an unwittingly comic aspect to Judas's outraged feelings:

53

At Bethany betimes my bale did begin
When Mary brought balm in a beauteous box
In t'best of all alabaster was t'balm brought in
And she lollopeth the lot on yon lotterell's locks!
(M, p. 99)

This is hardly a translation: it is a complete rewriting of the original
that retains some of its formal features (rhyme-scheme, alliteration)
but creates much greater metrical vitality and narrative substance. In
addition there is more emotional range and expressiveness – feelings
are enacted as well as simply described – and colloquial language
is fully exploited for comic effect, as in that wonderful pseudo-
medieval 'lollopeth'. Another such speech is that of the Woman in
the 'Palace of Cayphas' section. The York text has the 'Mulier' say
to Peter:

Than gaynesaies thou here the sawes that thou saide,
  How he schulde claim to be callid God sonne,
And with the workis that he wrought whils he walked
  Baynly at our bydding alway to be bonne.
(no. 26, ll. 123–6)

Harrison's rewriting of this has a relentless, hammering insistence
that drives home the magnitude of Peter's denial of Jesus:

Then hen heart avow all ye averred was amiss
When ye said that yon sawterell shall save us from sin
And gainsay that that gadling God's given son is
Who walketh the world all wights' worship to win.
(M, p. 115)

Comparison of *The Mysteries* with any of their pageant-play originals
will yield many such examples of Harrison's skill. Whether in local
details or in the larger patterns made by careful editing and the
deployment of the Band, with its songs and choric commentary,
Harrison has fashioned a theatrical edifice that may come to stand
for a long time as a fulfilment of what the original cycles were

54

separately and partially striving for. In any case, *The Mysteries* is one of his best attempts to honour the thwarted and often forgotten creative energies of the unnamed common people of the North of England from whom he has sprung.

A far less reassuring treatment of the common people's creativity is to be found in *The Trackers of Oxyrhynchus*. Containing, as it does, both the Delphi and National Theatre texts, the 1991 Faber edition of this play provides a unique opportunity to identify the changes that were made between its first performance in Greece and the revised version that was performed in London and at Salt's Mill in Bradford. In terms of content, the earlier text is more conscious of its Greek setting and more scrupulous in providing historical and other scholarly information. For example, a full half of Grenfell's long opening speech is taken up with references to the pioneering archaeological work of Flinders Petrie, whereas its Mark 2 version has no reference whatsoever to Petrie, or to Grenfell's early career. The Delphi text also contains many more quotations from and references to classical Greek literature, including the whole of Pindar's 'Paean for the People of Delphi' in the original, and much greater use of extracts from the fragmentary satyr play of Sophocles (called the *Ichneutae*, 'The Trackers') which provided the inspiration and shape for most of what happens in both of Harrison's versions. Most often the second version looks more concise and more theatrically effective than the first; for example, Silenus's speech on pages 26 and 94 and Grenfell/Apollo's long speech on pages 22–5 and 91–3. Moreover, greater theatrical effectiveness is usually associated with a sharper political focus. Take a late section from Silenus's long speech about the flaying of his brother Marsyas and his own acceptance of cultural subordination.

Delphi version:

> I didn't mind a bit of inferior status
> as long as there was Bacchus to inebriate us.
> I didn't mind a bit of lowly forelock-tugging
> as long as it went with retsina-glugging.
> To social inequality I turned a blind eye
> if that guaranteed the liquor supply.
> Some sort of pattern seemed to exist,
> get a bit pissed on then go and get pissed.
> I didn't mind conniving with gods and their greed

if my modest wants were guaranteed.
Unlike my poor flayed brother, Marsyas,
I never yearned to move out of my class.
Better we satyrs stay where we are
with Bacchus at least there's a buckshee bar.

(SILENUS tries to drink again from his wineskin and finds
it empty. He begins to pick over the rubbish mounds for
discarded beer cans.)

I'm a happy horse/human, half and half.
Maybe I'd like less hair on my calf,
my features might be a little less coarse
more of the human and less of the horse.
But unlike brother Marsyas I don't aspire
to master the flute or play on the lyre.
In short, I suppose, I'm not really averse
to being a satyr. I could do a lot worse.

(To CHORUS)

So don't make waves, boys. Don't rock the boat.
And add up the pluses of being man/goat.

(TO, p. 69)

National Theatre version:

So I don't make waves. I don't rock the boat.
I add up the plusses of being man/goat.
Unlike my poor flayed brother, Marsyas,
I've never yearned to move out of my class.
In short, I suppose, I'm not really averse
to being a satyr. I could do a lot worse.
I just have to find the best way to exist
and I've found, to be frank, I exist best pissed.

(p. 126)

The superiority of the later version should be obvious: the relentless
accumulation of booze-images in version one ('Bacchus . . . inebriate

us . . . retsina-glugging . . . liquor supply . . . get pissed . . . buckshee bar') is pared down to the consonantal minefield in which the cost of giving in and its attendant drunken speech problems are summed up in version two: 'I exist best pissed'. The rhetoric of resignation is more poignantly clear when it is freed from the pyrotechnics that surround and stifle it in version one: the clichés are fewer, but more prominent, and all of them are applied by Silenus to himself. His shamefaced comparison of his own capitulation with his brother's creative daring, 'I never yearned to move out of my class', stands more rawly revealed when it is not hobbled by the· redundant amplifications that follow it for a further eight lines in version one. Version one is too anxious to explain and to analyse, instead of letting the truth of the character's predicament emerge from his attempts to evade it. Detached assessments like 'I didn't mind conniving with gods and their greed/ if my modest wants were guaranteed' only interfere with our sense of how thoroughly (at this stage) Silenus is morally disabled by his acquiescence in the gods' hegemony. Much more compelling is the attempt at a succinct summary (i.e. evasion of the challenge) of his situation, given a Prufrockian dimension in version two by the addition of a final 'to be frank' to the previous 'In short, I suppose . . .'.

In *The Trackers of Oxyrhynchus*, more than in any other of his plays, Harrison has tackled issues closest to those in his most political non-theatrical verse. Silenus and his fellow satyrs are clog-shod proletarians whose creative energy is banished to the margins of art, though the original satyr play was as integral to the cultural vision of Athenian Greece as the trilogy of tragedies that always preceded it in performance. Harrison's anger at the exclusion of the working class from official 'high' culture (the age-old antagonism of 'them' towards '[uz]') is admirably embodied in the cocky intellectualism of Apollo and the uncompromising snootiness of Kyllene. But the collective history represented by the satyrs is at the very centre of the play, and here again the second version is better in a number of crucial respects. It breaks up several of the more static individual satyr speeches of the Delphi text and turns them into a more choric, more truly communal, form of expression; so that

KYLLENE

Dead it has a voice. Alive it was dumb.

SATYR 11
Give us a clue. Is it bent, fat, short or what?

KYLLENE
'Tis spotted and shaped somewhat like a pot.

SATYR 12
A leopard, of course, or some sort of cat.

KYLLENE
No, sorry. It isn't at all like that.
(*TO*, p. 42)

becomes:

KYLLENE
Dead it has a voice. Alive it was dumb.

CHORUS OF SATYRS
All
Give us a clue.
C9
Is it bent,
C8
fat,
C7
short,
All
or what?

KYLLENE
'Tis spotted and shaped somewhat like a pot.

CHORUS OF SATYRS
A2
A leopard,
All
of course,
A 1, 3

58

or some sort of cat.

KYLLENE

No, sorry. It's nothing at all like that.

(pp. 108–9)

Kyllene's single voice is much more strikingly counterpointed by the cascading components of a common voice in the second version. Compare also the responses to Apollo's first seductive performance on the lyre:

Delphi version:

SATYR 1

Oh, it's wonderful. Let me have a go!
I'd love to try it out.   (*TO*, p. 54)

National Theatre version:

CHORUS OF SATYRS

All

Oh, it's wonderful. Let us have a go!

(*TO*, p. 119)

Another instance, small but significant, of how individuals are assimilated to a collective experience that gives structure and coherence to its constituent elements.

That collective voice is finally transformed, in version two, into the shouted obscenities of graffiti-spraying satyr/hooligans angrily rejecting 'Apollonian art' in favour of a Dionysian piss-up in which Hermes's harp becomes Harp lager. In the Delphi text the 'hooligan' episode is played without speech, let alone the chanted 'fucks' of version two, and it soon modulates into an innocuous 'six-aside football match', followed by some last-minute stage business with a 'flaming World Cup' and the letters of Sophocles's name in Ancient Greek. Version two brilliantly exploits its National Theatre/Royal Festival Hall location with pointed references to the proximity of such élitist art venues to the squalor and hopelessness of cardboard city. The theatre audience itself is made to act the embarrassed unresponsiveness of the uncomprehending middle class through its inability to read aloud the scraps of papyri and thus help Silenus and his 'lads' begin their bid for a share of the cultural limelight. Version two's final image of Silenus slapped down by high art and silently screaming as he waits for Apollo's flayers is the most powerful political and theatrical image in all Harrison's dramatic work.

As I have just suggested, one strength of the National Theatre version of *The Trackers of Oxyrhynchus* is its use of highly charged contemporary issues like homelessness and vandalism. It even glances hilariously at the Tory National Curriculum and its probable impact on working-class children. Yet the social realities of the 1980s are given a greater prominence still in *The Common Chorus* (1992), which was written for the National Theatre just after *The Trackers* but is so far unperformed. It is a version of Aristophanes's *Lysistrata*, set at Greenham Common when the Women's Peace Camps were at their most active. Such close linkages to a precise historical phase of the anti-nuclear struggle left the play, in Harrison's own words, 'marooned in its moment' (*CC*, p. xvi) when the Cold War officially ended and the missiles, with their American minders, were withdrawn. Nevertheless, the play has resonances that are not quite so vulnerable to the military policy changes of the late eighties and early nineties. Certainly, the gender relations represented in it are meshed with the specifics of the Greenham camps and missile base, as when the three guards stand self-consciously behind model phalluses, fashioned by the women, which also resemble cruise missiles. But this image, and all those directly linking masculine sexual potency and arousal with militarism and violence, clearly prompt the reader/spectator to invoke a long and depressing history of such reciprocal connections. Integral to the play's structure is a constant interaction between past and present in which the Greenham women have to keep reminding themselves whether they are in 1980s Britain or the Athens of 411 BC. Unfortunately, this formal strategy has some serious limitations.

In his introduction to *The Common Chorus*, Harrison quotes from Caroline Blackwood's first-hand account of life at the Peace Camps, *On the Perimeter* (1984). In the last chapter of that very informative book, Blackwood makes some comparisons between the Greenham women and the women in *Lysistrata*:

> Both groups of women banded together and rejected men in order to protest the pointlessness of war, the waste of

national resources, the murder of their sons. Aristophanes' play was a comedy and he could resolve the male–female conflict light-heartedly. The play that was being enacted on Greenham Common had no such easy resolution, and it had undertones that were not comic. (pp. 108–9)

Harrison acknowledges this non-comic dimension when he speaks of trying to combine *Lysistrata* with Euripides's *The Trojan Women* in *The Common Chorus*. His Lysistrata speaks at times more like Hecuba than Aristophanes's heroine, but the play in which she appears is more a comedy than a tragedy, and it is in this respect that the issue of accuracy is uncomfortably raised. Once again, Blackwood provides a helpful focus:

> The Greenham women were quite prepared to take on all the hostility and derision that their role was traditionally bound to arouse. Scorn and hostility could neither ruffle nor deter them, just as it never deterred the suffragettes when English society considered them pathetic, unfeminine figures of fun as they chained themselves to the railings.
>
> The Greenham women had given up caring that they had the most disgusting public image. Many of their supporters wished they could be made to care more. They wished the young girls wouldn't paint their faces with webs and wear punk hair-styles. They wished the lesbians could be persuaded to be more restrained. But the peace women felt all these considerations were really immaterial and frivolous. What did it matter how they dressed? What did it matter what any of them were like as individuals? They had never claimed to be plaster saints. They were not trying to set fashions for *Vogue*. All that mattered was their position, which they believed to be a sane and pure one. (p. 36)

To the above should be added Blackwood's admiring comment on the camps' lack of hierarchy: 'There was no one in charge at the camps. No one ever told anyone else to do anything' (p. 16). Thus a picture is clearly drawn of a very democratic, serious-minded, sexually diverse group of women being daily (and nightly)

confronted by the most vicious and often obscene aggression from
the soldiers guarding the missiles, and from many local residents
as well. Whatever broad similarities Blackwood notes between
such modern women and those created by Aristophanes, there
are so many radical differences that a speech like the following,
by Lysistrata, is ludicrously wide of the mark:

> I can't keep them here. They're all in need of it.
> Prick-sick the lot of 'em. And ready to quit.
> They seemed so dedicated but they desert
> because their randy bodies are on Red Alert.
> Women behaving like those lot say they do –
> any little dodge to get themselves a screw.
> Those foul-mouthed louts behind their barricade
> are right: all women want is to get laid.
> Every little dodge, every devious trick,
> anything at all to get a dose of dick.
> Every kind of lie, every sneaky stratagem
> to get a stiff six inches into them.
> Every fraud you've heard of, every ruse,
> more concerned with cock than campaigning against Cruise.
> They're all so randy, so screaming for a screw
> it can't be long before the Peace Campaign is through.
> I found one by the Orange Gate trying to hitch
> a lift back to London, the treacherous bitch!
> One by the roadside skirt half up her thigh
> luring lorry drivers into a lay-by.
> There was even one about to sneak off to the bar
> where the US personnel take R & R.
> Women! Women! Traitors, they betray
> our campaign sisterhood for one quick lay.
>
> (*CC*, p. 61)

This is a close equivalent in tone to the original Lysistrata's
disillusionment with her fellow-campaigners. Its content, however,
is so specific to the Greenham situation that it demands comparison
with the reality as depicted by Blackwood. After every allowance
has been made for comic exaggeration, such a comparison can only
demonstrate that Harrison is much more faithful to Aristophanes.

than he is to Blackwood or, presumably, the Greenham women with
whom he spoke (*CC*, p. xiv). From Blackwood's account he takes
many circumstantial details, like the 'benders' and the face-painting,
but he flatly contradicts the most crucial elements of the picture she
presents.

The original Lysistrata and her comrades fought their sexual
battle against a very specific conflict, the Peloponnesian War,
which had dragged on for twenty-one years and in which their
menfolk were directly involved. Harrison's Lysistrata insists that in
the modern world such local wars are always in danger of escalating
into a global catastrophe:

> Since Hiroshima what we've done
> paradoxically's to make the whole world one.
> We all look down the barrel of the same cocked gun.
> One target, in one united fate
> nuked together in some hyperstate.
>
> (*CC*, p. 49)

The same long speech describes the women's previous political
docility:

> We've heard you men plan world-wide Apocalypse
> and we went on serving dinner with sealed lips.
> We went on sitting with our knitting in our laps
> while you moved model missiles on your maps.
> We heard the men's low murmur over their moussaka
> and knew the world's future was growing a lot darker.
> Serving the coffee we heard dark hints
> of coming holocaust with after-dinner mints.
> All this time supportive to the last
> we nailed our colours to the macho mast.
>
> (p. 50)

To bring his Greenham women as closely into line with their
Athenian counterparts as possible, Harrison represents them as
uniformly heterosexual, married, middle-class and previously non-
political. He also shows them as willing to play the glamourwear

catalogue prick-teaser in order to enforce their anti-war message, another example of where sticking close to Aristophanes produces a serious – and, to many Greenham women, insulting – travesty of what the Peace Campaign was all about. To be sure, the men in the play are systematically exposed as thugs and sexists. The egregious Inspector is even stripped by the women at one point to reveal female underwear under his uniform. Nevertheless, there is at the very least an awkward simplification in having the 1980s Lysistrata talk about other women as reductively as she does in the speech already quoted and in her exchange with the Inspector on pp. 54–5:

LYSISTRATA

Worse off than those women who have known
a little love and now are left alone,
's the girl, approaching womanhood, who waits
while war is wiping out all likely mates.

INSPECTOR

Men grow old, you know, not only you.

LYSISTRATA

Yes, but look what happens when you do.
Bald, decrepit, toothless a man still gets
into the knickers of nubile nymphettes.
But for a woman once she's over the hill . . .

The difficulty here, as elsewhere, is that the closer the text gets to Aristophanes the less it represents a credible, or even an amusing, version of what Greenham women were like and what their strategy was. Where the Greenham experience can be virtually forgotten, and the reader can concentrate on the verbal acrobatics and imagined stage business, the effect can be uproariously funny. Harrison works wonders with the great scene between Myrrhine and Kinesias, where Kinesias's desperate preoccupation with his erect penis produces gems like 'Up! Up! Can't you bloody see/ I've been up since seven. *He's* been up since three!' (p. 73). Such moments of straightforward comic gusto are few compared with the embarrassing maladroitness with which most of the story is handled.

It must be said that Harrison has often done his best to give women a quantitative fair deal in his theatre work. Apart from *The Common Chorus*, he has created or adapted prominent roles for women in *The Misanthrope*, *Phaedra Britannica* and *Medea: A Sex-War Opera*. If the all-male cast of *The Oresteia* was an attempted subversion of gender stereotyping, then the almost all-female cast of *Square Rounds* (1992) must be seen in the same light.[9] Furthermore, the plays and libretti contain explicit warnings about patriarchal prejudice and cruelty:

> Wives and mothers, always losers,
> women workers, husbands boozers.
> Women's work is never-ending,
> men's main work is . . . elbow-bending!
> (*The Bartered Bride*, *DV* and *TW*, p. 151)

> A woman is what men desert;
> in opera (as in life!) men hurt
> and harm her.
> (*Medea*, *DV* and *TW*, p. 369)

> As the sex-war's still being fought
> which sex does a myth support
> you should be asking.
> What male propaganda lurks
> behind most operatic works
> that music's masking?
> (*Medea*, *DV* and *TW*, p. 433)

Yet there is still a remarkable continuity between the misogyny of Palladas and Martial and the prevailing images of women offered by the theatre pieces. Célimène and Kyllene are supercilious and shallow; the Memsahib, Clytemnestra and Medea are gripped by destructive passions; in *Bow Down* the Fair Sister is pushed in the river because of female rivalry and her corpse is then robbed, sexually abused and grotesquely mutilated before it is finally turned into a harp. The Dark Sister is tortured to make her confess to her crime. As the rack is tightened, she utters the same words ('Sing I die, sing I day') as the Miller's Servant had shouted while ejaculating into his drawers at the prospect of fucking the Fair Sister's corpse.

This is the most extreme example of a general tendency to accord women none of the sympathy or respect that they receive in poems like 'The Nuptial Torches', 'Following Pine' and 'Cypress and Cedar'. At their best they are recalcitrant and irrational, at their worst masochistic and murderous. Tributes to the creativity and courage of the common people – most notably in *The Mysteries* and *Trackers* – are an important counterweight to such 'masculine myopia',[10] but they should not be allowed to excuse it altogether. Harrison has insisted: 'It's not that I glory in what happens in the plays, because I think the crushing of the female principle is one of the great shortcomings of society in England and beyond . . . '[11] Perhaps it is the very notion of a 'female principle' itself that helps to relegate women so often to the realm of sex, as predators or victims, in Harrison's work.

'The School of Eloquence':
silence and history

> The inarticulate, by definition, leave few
> records of their thoughts.
> (Edward Thompson)

With the publication of *From 'The School of Eloquence' and other poems* (1978) and its extended sequel, *Continuous* (1981), Harrison's work took a considerable stride forward in its ability to express political meanings. Some of the sixteen-line sonnets that make up the whole (as yet unfinished, potentially unfinishable) 'School' sequence have the compact symmetry and force of bullets fired in the class war. At the same time, many of them are also achingly poignant memories of a bright lad's – and successful man's – uneasy relationship with his uncomprehending working-class parents. The whole sequence draws together, and often dovetails, the political and the historical with the emotional and the biographical in its examination of issues like the estrangement caused by a bourgeois education and the generations-deep roots of class inequality and cultural deprivation. Above all, the unifying theme is that of 'eloquence' itself; more specifically, of how a command of language can liberate, and its absence imprison.

'The School of Eloquence' is taken from E.P. Thompson's seminal study of emergent class consciousness *The Making of the English Working Class* (1963). It refers to the radicalism of the late-eighteenth-century Corresponding Societies, organisations harassed to extinction as the state grew more and more fearful of French Jacobinism and its British counterparts. The quotation from Thompson which serves as epigraph to the whole sequence identifies the learning of eloquence as a vital element in the education of radical artisans. For men like John Binns (an 'indefatigable conspirator', according to Thompson[1]) there could be no real social change without the linguistic means to mobilise people *en masse*, and to educate them as individuals. Yet eloquence alone was not enough, for power lay overwhelmingly with those who had wealth, status and a developed class identity; for example, those who could – and did – pass legislation 'utterly suppressing and prohibiting' the London Corresponding Society, of which Binns was a prominent member. The necessity of eloquence and the education that goes with it are thus set squarely alongside the realities of political power, which can be made to change (if at all) only by a radicalism as active in deed as in word.

For Harrison, however, the challenge of a radical discourse is complicated and confused by his own hard-earned education. What can the Classics graduate from Leeds University make of the inarticulate, but undeniably radical, utterances of the class warriors of an earlier generation? 'On Not Being Milton', the first poem in the sequence, declares its radical sympathies in its dedication to two Frelimo activists; yet the poem itself is a dizzying display of ingenuity that turns in upon its own significance to the point of self-extinction. It advances by a series of contradictions: (a) it is 'committed to the flames', yet is palpably before our eyes; (b) it is an act of humility by someone trying to reclaim a proletarian cultural inheritance (the class equivalent of the *négritude* affirmed in Aimé Césaire's poem 'Cahier d'un retour au pays natal'), yet its language is dense with lexical difficulty from the reference to Gray's 'Elegy' in the title, via the French phrase, to the linguistic terms 'glottals' and 'morphemes'; (c) it celebrates 'mute ingloriousness' and 'articulation', so that the final quotation from Tidd the Cato Street conspirator[2] is chosen both because it is barely literate, and because its very inarticulateness is rich in unconscious significance – 'Righting' is, after all, what radicalism is all about. The central tension throughout is that between the 'Ludding' impulse to smash the 'frames of Art' and the fact – so blatantly foregrounded – that the 'looms of . . . language' are now 'owned' as much by Harrison himself as by the ruling class.[3]

Much less self-defeating is the first of the two poems that make up 'The Rhubarbarians'. Here the text mobilises its Ludding phonemes – a gang of glottals, plosives and dentals – to represent the Yorkshire croppers' attacks on mills in 1812 as a contest between speech and action. The mill-owners had their words faithfully transcribed, whereas the croppers were relegated to a 'rhubarb' – muttering mob of extras in the scenario constructed by the ruling-class record. It is the poem's task to liberate the meaning of action ('the *tusky-tusky* of the pikes') from the enforced silence of history. Demotic abbreviations, strongly emphasised at the fractured beginnings of two widely separated lines (''d've liked' and ''s silence'), show the class struggle being waged between the grammar of proletarian radicalism and the law and order of bourgeois prosodic form: they insist upon the integrity of the croppers' experience (and its continuity with the rest of working-class history) as something that wrenches at and threatens to pull apart the constraints of the text's very traditional structure. The same battle goes on in terms of rhythm and rhyme: the four or five stresses per line are constantly jostled around and interspersed with varying numbers of unstressed syllables; the rhyme-scheme at last gives way under pressure as the final stanza resolves itself into a pair of rhyming couplets that enact the Luddites' hard-won solidarity.

The second poem of the pair moves away from the terrain of collective history (where Thompson is the Virgil to Harrison's Dante) and into that of autobiography. It is an arch, self-conscious performance, one that marks the furthest extremity of failure in the whole sequence. Where the companion poem had appropriated 'rhubarb' as a means of focusing the historic conflict between words and silence, here we are offered a series of slick variations which domesticate the same word to Harrison's complacent view of his own profession. George Formby's inanely cheerful rendering of working-class experience is an apt epigraph to such a text: it anticipates the condescension that characterises Harrison's attitude towards his father:

> Sorry, dad, you won't get that quatrain.
> (I'd like to be the poet my father reads!)
> *(SP*, p. 114)

After an opening stanza about the difficulty of translating Smetana's Czech, this apology rings hollow, though not as hollow as the bracketed assurance that Harrison would, above all, like to earn his father's understanding and respect. In its attempt at a closure that can contain Harrison's loyalty to his father (and, of course, his father's *class*) while never seriously challenging his accelerating professional success, rhubarb (the vegetable and the noise) provides a bridge from the two lines quoted above into the series of tropes (musical notation, young rhubarb shoots, operatic choruses, audiences' applause) that take us up to the final spectacle of the Leeds lad mockingly exacting respect from the New York cultural establishment.

Harrison senior's commonplace statement about Leeds being the rhubarb-growing capital of England is enlisted as a piece of earthy paternal realism to which the clever son can defer as evidence of his genuine desire for mutual understanding. That realism is then directed against the grandiose absurdity of 'arias, duets, quartets' and the Met Set's highbrow enthusiasm. However, there is a limit to how far Harrison's mockery can go. Biting the hands that clap him is one thing; rejecting art (his own and Smetana's and the Metropolitan Opera Company's) is something else. Thus the operatic songs are allowed to 'soar to precision from our common tongue', a formulation that asserts the unifying universality (common-ness) of language (his father's, Smetana's and his own) even as it relegates ordinary (common) language to a position below that achieved – and achievable – by operatic libretti. It is no wonder that Harrison's historical understanding begins to waver when he turns to his own ambiguous position. The classical scholar and internationally known writer is vulnerable to charges of what he himself calls 'busk[ing] the class' (in 'Turns') if what he writes reads finally like an attempt to add a savour of proletarian irony to the sweet taste of establishment recognition.[4]

Although 'The Rhubarbarians, II' makes us question the productiveness with which Harrison's 'art is at war with its own medium',[5] his strategy of denigrating the formal and linguistic means by which his meaning is fashioned does not always betray him into factitious ingenuity. When his subject is not himself – when it is chosen primarily for its social rather than autobiographical significance – the effect can be very powerful. 'Working' presents the plight of one female victim of the Industrial Revolution whose testimony was recorded by the Children's Employment Commission in 1842, and is quoted by Thompson.[6] Harrison reduces Patience Kershaw's age from the seventeen of the Commission's Report to a more vulnerable fourteen, and adds details like 'You've been underneath too long to stand the light'; but such alterations and additions in no way falsify the representative character of the girl's experience. In any case, the poem is about not only the girl herself but also the necessity of rescuing her from the mass grave of historical neglect to which so many like her were consigned:

> this wordshift and inwit's a load of crap
> for dumping on a slagheap, I mean
> *th'art nobbut summat as wants raking up.*
>
> . . .
>
> Wherever hardship held its tongue the job
> 's breaking the silence of the worked-out gob.
>
> (*SP*, p. 124)

A footnote to the poem explains that 'gob' is 'an old Northern coal-mining word for the space left after the coal has been extracted. Also, of course, the mouth and speech.' Patience Kershaw's own gob was silenced by the harsh conditions of labour underground: the poem's *raison d'être* is to liberate the significance of her suffering from the inarticulateness of her subterranean existence. In her Harrison has found an object for his imaginative appropriation that advances his political understanding: the more the girl's experience is articulated, the more it is grasped in its historical as well as personal reality. The text achieves a unity of theory (politics) and practice (poetry) which itself represents the true alternative to what, for the girl, was an inescapable destiny. The act of imaginative recuperation becomes an assertion of transhistorical solidarity. Herbert Marcuse's words can serve to summarise the importance of what Harrison is engaged in here: 'The wounds that heal in time are also the wounds that contain the poison. Against this surrender to time, the restoration of remembrance to its rights, as a vehicle of liberation, is one of the noblest tasks of thought.'[7]

The same unmistakable commitment is evident in a group of other poems which, together with 'Working', may be taken to represent the core of Harrison's achievement in the first *'School of Eloquence'* collection. 'Classics Society', 'National Trust' and 'Them & [uz], I and II' all manage to take firm imaginative hold of the historical significance (in other words, *the class content*) of personal experience. The old boy of Leeds Grammar School pays ironic tribute to the classical education which has been such a powerful instrument of ruling-class hegemony in Britain:

> The tongue our leaders use to cast their spell
> was once denounced as 'rude', 'gross', 'base' and 'vile'
> How fortunate we are who've come so far!
>
> ('Classics Society', *SP*, p. 120)

Yet the triumph of English over Latin as the medium of official public discourse did not oust the conservatism of classics teaching, with its emphasis upon slavish imitation of Cicero's style. As a means of enforcing conformity and encouraging the view that getting 'the alphas' is best accomplished by not deviating from the prescribed model, classics, as taught at Leeds Grammar School at least as late as when Harrison went there, remained very effective. The principal function of such teaching was, of course, ideological: it was an indispensable discipline for those whose role would be to oversee a divided society. Thus, finding 'good Ciceronian for Burke's:/ *a dreadful schism in the British nation*' is, in reality, a strategy for neutralising the vernacular urgency and relevance of the warning itself.

Being subjected to such conditioning was doubly ironic for boys like Harrison: it happened at two removes from their ordinary speech, since the kind of English they were translating out of or into was, after all, the English of the middle class – of Hansard and the British Empire – not that of their homes or neighbourhoods. That it should be the reactionary Burke whose words were to be translated only reinforces the political character of the 'education' process. To render still safer the already safe utterances of an arch-apologist of state legality is a perfect instance of the ruling class's thoroughness in emasculating oppositional thought.[8]

'National Trust' begins with a horrifying example of how 'upholders of our law and order' abused the 'trust' that was placed in them by using a convict to test the depth of a mine-shaft at Castleton in Derbyshire. However, the critical focus then shifts to the role of scholars in writing such scandals out of the historical record. The whole story of how Cornish tin-miners were robbed of their labour, their native language and the chance to organise themselves into a prototype trade union is a bigger instance of the same abuse of others' rights by those with the power to control the means of collective expression and self-definition:

> The dumb go down in history and disappear
> and not one gentleman's been brought to book:
>
> *Mes den hep tavas a-gollas y dyr*
>
> (Cornish) – 'The tongueless man gets his land took.'
>
> (*SP*, p. 121)

No gentleman has been 'brought to book' because no gentleman's crimes have been recorded *in* a book. But the silence of the scholars (their *trahison des clercs*, which 'plumbs the depths' of the state's perfidy) is a very different thing from the tonguelessness of the miners: the first serves the interests of its exponents and their paymasters; the other is the most fundamental of dispossessions.

'Them & [uz]' is dedicated to 'Professors Richard Hoggart & Leon Cortez' – the first a Leeds-born academic analyst of working-class culture; the second a comedian famous for his plebeian mangling of high culture, especially Shakespeare. The 'αιαι' of Demosthenes is transformed into the 'ayay!' with which Cortez and other stand-up comics greeted their audiences. Like them, Harrison was treated as an object of laughter. At school he was confined to playing the Porter in *Macbeth*, and told that only Received Pronunciation was suitable for reading Keats aloud or performing the poetic parts of Shakespeare.

By a clever deployment of the phonetic alphabet, to differentiate between the RP version of 'us' and Harrison's flattened vowel and soft 's', the text simultaneously dramatises the details of the boy's victimisation and establishes the credentials which authorise his contempt for his teacher-tormentor. Daniel Jones, the 'dozing' (superannuated, inattentive) author of a widely used dictionary of pronunciation,[9] is ridiculed not only because of his anti-working-class bias, but also because of his ignorance. Harrison scores his points against him through having become the better scholar and thus having beaten Jones at his own game. He has realised the implications of Keats's having been a Cockney; he has discovered that Wordsworth's vowels were as flat as his own; he has learnt the phonetic alphabet. Yet there is none of the complacency here that disfigures 'The Rhubarbarians, II'. The intellectual stance is neither arrogantly apologetic nor coyly self-parading. Instead, the scholarly pride is dovetailed with the class consciousness; for what purpose does the scrupulously accurate historical and linguistic information serve, if not that of advancing the claim to respect of Harrison's class? When he chews up 'Littererchewer'[10] and asserts his right to be called by his name and not his initials, he is striking a blow for something more than personal recognition.

It would clearly be a mistake to read these two poems as some kind of declaration of revolutionary faith. Nevertheless, the positive beliefs which they imply – in mutual respect in the pursuit of knowledge; in teaching that does not legitimise class condescension – could be the basis of larger, more radical commitments. The second poem is poised (irresolutely?) between, on the one hand, a *ressentiment* that hungers to appropriate and transform the whole terrain of poetry as a deliberate class manoeuvre and, on the other, a rueful retrospect by someone already inducted into the class which was responsible for the earlier humiliations. Beginning with the colloquial robustness of 'So right, yer buggers, then. We'll occupy/ your lousy leasehold poetry', it sustains a defiant posture until the last two lines, where the previous authority, derived from superior *knowledge*, is overlaid with an oblique but unmistakable reference to social success. Even 'one mention in the *Times*' is a symptom of enhanced status which shifts the balance of the poem towards a Hoggart-like emphasis on making the grade (with or without one's original accent intact) and away from questions about the nature and value of 'the grade' itself. We are now moving into the realm of Hoggart's deracinated 'scholarship boy'; but before we leave 'Them & [uz]', it should be said that there is much to enjoy in the poems' insubordinate gusto. Liberty-taking lines like 'R.I.P. R.P. R.I.P. T.W.' go a long way towards fulfilling the threat at the beginning of number II: if poetry is not completely 'occupied', it has certainly been subjected to a salutary raid or two.

'Study' and 'Me Tarzan' are separate but matching poems that deal with the problems of homework for would-be scholarship winners. 'Study' is particularly ironic, because nothing could be further from the conventional idea of a study than the room in which generations of such children, male and female, have had to do their studying. The peculiar lifelessness of a room kept only for special occasions, usually those connected with illness and death, has an inhibiting effect on the young Harrison: 'I try to whistle in it but I can't'. The 'dead' language the boy is reading is more stimulating than all the evidence of human activity (and its absence) in the room. Yet, despite its inhospitable atmosphere, the 'best room' supplies the silence upon which the boy's mind 'moves' in its search for knowledge. A greater problem is the attraction of 'laikin' with the other boys instead of poring over *De Bello Gallico*:

> It's only his jaw muscles that he's tensed
> into an enraged *shit* that he can't go;
> down with all polysyllables, he's against
> all pale-face Caesars, *for* Geronimo.
> ('Me Tarzan', *SP*, p. 116)

Richard Hoggart's account fits Harrison's situation perfectly: 'He is . . . likely to be separated from the boys' groups outside the home, is no longer a full member of the gang which clusters round the lamp-posts in the evenings; there is homework to be done.'[11]

The 'scholarship boy's' academic success is bought first at the cost of foregone peer-group camaraderie, and then at the more extortionate cost of estrangement from parents. That problem is confronted most movingly in 'Book Ends', where books provide the perfect figure for all that obstructs communication between father and son. Bereavement throws their mutual silence into sharper, almost unbearable relief: Harrison is helpless before the grief of his 'shattered' father; neither of them can give the other anything but company to see the night through drinking whisky. It had been the mother's role to remind them of how similar they were, 'like book ends' either side of the grate. She supplied the image that gave their tenuous relationship a fragile coherence and cohesion. Now her death has removed even that comforting fiction, and they are left wordless before the twin enormities of her absence and the insurmountable obstacle of Harrison's education. The crowding together of three lines in the final stanza enacts the accumulation of book-learning that has set a wall between the pair of them; for, when all is *not* said and done: 'what's between's/ not the thirty or so years, but books, books, books'.

'Book Ends' testifies to one major ironic consequence of education for the scholarship boy – that it can generate inhibited silence as

75

easily as liberated speech within the family. If silence is the condition of the dispossessed whom history has overlooked, it can also seep into the widening fissure between father and son as the boy doggedly acquires the means of greater self-expression and social recognition. Whatever the tragic ironies of such a predicament within any particular family, there is no fundamental paradox involved in it. The kind of learning dispensed by the original School of Eloquence was part of a collective project directed towards the emancipation of a whole emergent class. To be sure, it was undertaken by a radical minority; but it was conceived – and often practised – as the education of families, not of isolated, 'academic' individuals.[12]

In complete contrast to this, Harrison's induction into a thoroughly élitist grammar-school ethos of the late 1940s requires separation from domestic life as a first condition of its success. The scholarship boy 'has to be more and more alone, if he is going to "get on"'.[13] Hoggart does not consider the kind of deep estrangement that happens between Harrison and his father; he is more concerned with the scholarship boy's difficulties in negotiating the pitfalls of the institutional environment, together with the uneasy embourgeoisement which institutional acceptance involves. Nevertheless, he constantly acknowledges the perplexed, ambivalent, often downright miserable experience of being the 'clever one' in a working-class family. And for Harrison there is, of course, the added irony of his being a student of 'dead' languages which come to life for him in inverse ratio to the decline of the 'living' language he has shared with his father – and his mother. 'Wordlists, II' bemoans

> . . . the tongue that once I used to know
> but can't bone up on now, and that's mi mam's.
>
> (*SP*, p. 118)

Another dimension to the familial (though not the Harrison family's) mediation of social and political conditions is the married couple's experience, in 'Cremation', of the very inequalities by which Patience Kershaw and the Cornish miners were more nakedly oppressed. The poem dovetails the wordlessness of the materially and culturally impoverished with the dignified reticence of two people between whom much can be communicated without recourse to speech. It is a precise pattern of suggestion, which neither overlooks the pervasiveness of disease, exhaustion and insecurity (all of which are directly traceable to the husband's conditions of work as a coal-miner) nor pretends that the couple's fierce, unspoken mutual dependence is in any way reducible to a conjuncture of cultural determinants:

> A grip from behind that seems to mean *don't go*
> tightens through bicep till the fingers touch.
> His, his dad's and *his* dad's lifetime down below
> crammed into one huge nightshift, and too much.
>
> (*SP*, p. 125)

That nervous groping after sense – what the grip 'seems to mean' – is simultaneously an instance of inarticulateness and a moving demonstration of the couple's alertness to every nuance of each other's behaviour. A similar indissoluble linkage of the social and the personal occurs in the last two lines, where historical exploitation is rendered as a cumulative family tragedy in which the husband must play his allotted part. The placing of this poem immediately after 'Working' and before 'Book Ends' adds further weight to its emphasis on the shifting interface between history and biography.

The sound of silence becomes deafening in the poem's last six lines:

> He keeps back death the way he keeps back phlegm
> in company, curled on his tongue. Once left alone
> with the last coal fire in the smokeless zone,
> he hawks his cold gobful at the brightest flame,
> too practised, too contemptuous to miss.
>
> Behind the door she hears the hot coals hiss.
>
> (*SP*, p. 125)

The phlegm which prevents speech proves to be an eloquent expression of the husband's silent, absorbed struggle with his impending death. Coal, which provides the heat and light at the centre of family life, is also the source of the man's lung disease, so that his spitting at 'the brightest flame' is more than a mere display of accuracy: it is a gesture of defiance towards the industry that has destroyed his health as the price of fuelling his hearth. The fire that 'cremates' the phlegm in the last line becomes a final figure for the complex interactions of work and family life. It mitigates nothing of the working class's historical impoverishment, yet it also shows their lives as active centres of feeling where the struggles are such as will never be wholly susceptible to collective definitions or collective solutions.

Silence, speech and writing are related to each other and to issues of survival and social responsibility in 'The Earthen Lot' and 't'Ark'. (The poem that comes between them, 'History Classes', is a slight piece that Harrison sensibly dropped from *Continuous*, but it surfaces again in *Selected Poems*.) 'The Earthen Lot' refers both to death as a common human destiny (the lot of those on earth) and to a particular group of craftsmen – presumably stonemasons and engravers – whose occupation was regarded by the middle class as extremely menial and coarse ('earthy'). The epigraph, from William Morris, speaks of them as 'that oppressed and neglected herd of men' whose influence on buildings can be seen 'from Isphahan to Northumberland'. The poem contrasts their eroding graves and gravestones with the secure resting-places of 'their betters', buried in the lee of the Northumberland church, and thus sheltered from wind and sea. There is also clearly a reference to the Church as an institution which protects the wealthy and consigns the workers to oblivion. But the erosion of the 'formal Roman letters' provides a trope for the creative potentialities which their work and religion have suppressed in the masons: 'calligraphic Persian odes,/ singing of sherbet, sex in Samarkand'. Their 'responsibilities for others' dreams' have confined them to expressing the aspirations of their betters, instead of formulating their own and thereby ensuring for themselves a more permanent place in history.

Survival is a more problematical affair in 't'Ark'. Silence and speech are seen as intimately related: the closer language gets to silence ('extinction') the better it represents the destructive nihilism of human beings. The question is raised as to whether silence may be a more appropriate 'reserve' (both 'reticence' and 'haven') for a threatened world than language which, by 'numbering' things, only bears witness to – and may even encourage – their eventual destruction. Poetry also has a kind of reserve; it may be too reticent about what is happening in the wider world by sticking to its own self-limited territory. What matters most is an active linguistic engagement with the way the world is: even 'crushed people's talk' is preferable to no talk at all. It is better to go on celebrating (in the 'numbers' of poetry) the diversity of life, including languages, than to acquiesce mutely in the global carnage by not even bearing witness to what is being lost.

A terminal expedient may even be to resurrect a dead language (Latin) and an ancient Welsh verse-form (*cynghanedd*) to commemorate the passing of languages and animals alike. The poem itself becomes an ark that preserves at least the names of things; it offers a kind of ironic survival to the doomed, and a dark testimony to the much-abused covenant between the human race and its material home. Harrison's introduction to his translation of Palladas underlines the importance, for him, of not letting things disappear without comment: 'What is unique and even invigorating about Palladas is that there is no sense at all of "gracious" surrender either to the inevitability of death or to historical change.'[14] Though it is by no means as sardonic as Palladas's epigrams, 't'Ark' shows the same determination to keep talking while the ship goes down.

With the publication of *Continuous* in 1981, Harrison unveiled the three-part structure on which his growing sonnet sequence would henceforth be organised. Blake Morrison describes it thus:

> The intimate commemorative family poems of Part II are preceded by the densely-wrought politico-historical poems of Part I and followed by a looser set of poems (about politics, history, art and morality) in Part III . . . [15]

Morrison goes on to assert (rightly) that the elegies in Part Two are both supported and enhanced by their placing within a contextualising historical perspective. At the same time he points out that the balance between the politico-historical and the familial has shifted significantly since the first collection and that the shift is later consolidated in *Selected Poems* (1984), where the numbers of poems per part are: Part One, 14; Part Two, 35; Part Three, 18 (67 in all, though Morrison, strangely, counts only 64). In the second edition of *Selected Poems* (1987), Part Two is further expanded to 46, with no increase in either of the other parts. This enhanced concentration on the familial is signalled in *Continuous* (and, again, in *Selected Poems*) by the addition of an epigraph from Milton's Latin poem 'Ad Patrem', which is both a tribute to a father 'worthy of all reverence', from whom the poet's gifts have sprung, and a prayer that the father's memory may be best preserved for posterity in the language of his dutiful son.

In contrast to the paternal encouragement Milton received, Harrison adds another epigraph which comically explains his talent as either a simple 'mystery' or an aberration akin to the stammering and speechlessness of his uncles Joe and Harry. Morrison comments: 'The poet's inheritance, this epigraph implies, is linguistic struggle, awkward articulacy, "mute ingloriousness" . . .'.[16] These are unquestionably part of his inheritance, but they do not account for his becoming a poet. Though Harrison later allows some warrant for Morrison's reading,[17] I prefer a comic confession of bafflement at the sheer arbitrariness of it all – dumbness to Harry; poetic talent to Tony. After all, the whole thrust of the 'School' sequence is against the notion that people become articulate merely because they inherit deprivation. What rescues them is collective struggle and/or an individual talent that may or may not be allowed to develop, and most probably will not be. With a characteristic Yorkshire poker face, Harrison offers an 'explanation' of his talent that slyly endorses the questioner's own assumption about the strangeness of juxtaposing two such concepts as 'working-class' and 'poet'. Even stammering and dumbness would be more 'natural' forms of aberration in a class historically deprived of the means of effective self-expression.

The twenty sonnets added to 'Book Ends' and 'A Close One' in Part Two of *Continuous* amplify enormously the Harrison family's experience and that of their neighbourhood. To the original 'Book Ends' is attached a companion poem which takes us beyond the silence of mutual hopelessness to the challenge of composing lapidary verse to express the father's love for his dead wife. Harrison is unable, after all, to find a superior alternative to his father's clichés – their sincerity is unimprovable. (Similarly, in 'Blocks' the poet son is reluctant to deliver a speech about his mother's life and death: his linguistic skill is not up to unblocking his own feelings and hauling the appropriate words into place.)

Equally sincere, though more questionable, are the racial attitudes attributed to Harrison senior in a number of poems. 'Next Door, I' introduces his fear of being 't'only white' left in the street; 'III' acknowledges that 'You *try* to understand: *Their sort don't know.*/ They're from the sun. But wait till they're old men.' It is not until number IV, however, that the old man's bewilderment and outrage are fully articulated in a series of protests about the neighbourhood being 'taken over' and the traditional white working-class culture obliterated. This is a creditable attempt to allow the father's feelings their due weight, but the poem's conclusion is worryingly noncommittal:

> Last of the 'old lot' still left in your block.
> Those times, they're gone. The 'old lot' can't come back.
>
> Both doors I notice now you double lock –
>
> he's already in your shoes, your next-door black.
>
> (SP, p. 132)

The last line suggests that there may be continuities of insecurity and embattled conservatism that transcend racial differences; but the reading most forcefully suggested by the poem as a whole is that of black people as a collective threat, even if the 'next-door black' is himself threatened by the changes that are taking place. The reality of cultural change is more fairly dealt with in *v.* (see pp. 96–7 below). Here the 'decline' of older working-class communities is too readily allowed to be the result of an Asian and Afro-Caribbean influx; the father's authentic unhappiness is too easily accepted as a validation of his ignorance and prejudice. Harrison is able to dissociate himself from such a view only when he is not dealing directly with his father's feelings: 'Clearing, II' exhorts the now-dead father to 'Bless this house's new black owners . . .', an awkward but safe substitute for challenging the father's racism when he was alive.

It would be fatuous to expect Harrison to refute his father's prejudices point by point, or even to insert somewhere a declaration of his own liberal principles: there must be scope for allowing the father's feelings to declare themselves in all their emotional truth. Nevertheless, it is a potent irony that, in a sequence of poems so much about the enforced silence of the oppressed, black people should remain the voiceless objects of white suspicion or, at best, of white condescension. The ambivalence towards blacks which blunted the anti-colonial cutting edge of 'The White Queen'[18] re-emerges here as a reluctance to challenge working-class racism for fear of compromising the precarious identification of son with father. Harrison's persona is caught in a double bind both as son and as scholarship boy. It is a familiar one to many educated liberals (let alone socialists) of that generation, though that makes it no easier to deal with. For Harrison to face the full implications of his father's attitudes would further estrange them from each other; it would also require from him a wider and firmer grasp of the nature of inequality than his class perspective by itself can give him. Commemorating the sufferings of his own family and class is one thing; addressing the oppression to which blacks (or women, or gays) have been subject is something else.

Necessary as it is to identify the silences or evasions in poems so centrally concerned with the liberating power of speech, it is also important to acknowledge their frequent success in describing the deep emotional ties which make effective communication – let alone serious discussion – so difficult between parents and children. The title-poem, 'Continuous', movingly notes the ironic repetitions that link father to son from one generation to another. An inherited ring and the looped tape playing organ music at Harrison senior's cremation are figures for the inescapable continuities of family life, memory and habit. With little in common but a liking for James Cagney films (wordlessly watched, of course), Harrison father and son are none the less bound by an unspoken bond that may be attenuated but cannot finally be broken. Even in the furnace-fire that will consume the father,

. . . his father's ring will keep its shape.

I wear it now to Cagneys on my own.

(*SP*, p. 143)

Across three generations, and despite enormous gaps in understanding and sympathy, something persists. A crucial part of that process for Harrison is the memory that bears conscious witness to his minimal, but pervasive, patrimony. The memory of the choc ices his father bought him has survived the 'White Heat' of the furnace, though there is a simultaneous recognition of the father's undemonstrative nature which allowed him to show his feelings for the boy only in such simple, mute tokens of affection. At such a moment the deafening historical silence of the working class finds an echo in one man's repressed paternal emotion.

The father's death is a 'reticence' that 'crowns his life's' ('Turns'), a last 'release from mortal speech' ('Marked With D') for the man who never even mastered the ukelele as a means of self-expression or upward social mobility ('Punchline'). Death and cremation involve a whole series of ironic reflections on the limits within which both parents' lives were lived. The father, a baker by trade, ends up in an oven himself, though one in which – if only 'literally' – his tongue can 'burst into flame'. In 'Bringing Up', the mother would remain 'unreconciled' to *The Loiners*, even if the book had been burnt with her in the same fire and its ashes mingled with hers: her proletarian puritanism could never stomach her son's 'mucky' treatment of sexuality. The mother's wedding ring ('Timer'), like the grandfather's (in 'Continuous'), serves to epitomise what is permanent in the parents' legacy to their son, yet its failure to melt also mocks the father's conviction that he will one day be reunited with his wife in death.

Pentecostal fire and the effort of speech link cremation with eloquence in 'Fire-eater'. For the father and his stammerer brother (the Uncle Joe of the epigraph) the act of speaking was a species of painful conjuring whereby words were strung together and dragged into the light from 'deep down in their gut', a region alike of authentic feeling and tense inhibition. Now the ties of filiation require the son to fashion a string of his own that will both continue the family 'line' and supersede earlier speech acts by retying the grammatical knots and virtually reinventing a vocabulary to express the family's often unarticulated experience. Harrison must assume an Adamic role in shaping names that will bring order out of chaos, and thus ensure that the flames which consumed his parents become world-creating fire and also the fiery furnace from which an indestructible humanity can be rescued.

The first two poems of 'Illuminations' make brilliant use of Blackpool seaside images to characterise the family's 'loosening ties' as well as its inescapable connectedness. Despite the long history of mutual incomprehension and estrangement, there are moments of understanding and sympathy to record. The saddest irony of all is that the understanding is retrospective, and has come mostly after the parents' deaths. In a sense it has taken their deaths to 'illuminate' for their son the real strength of a bond that seemed so tenuous when they were alive. Moreover, for the atheist Harrison it is only in his own physical and psychological being that his parents can be said to have survived and been united: 'eternity, annihilation, me,/ that small bright charge of life where they both meet'. In the third poem it is once again silence – the unspoken and the unutterable – that most emphatically represents the family's spirit-sapping tensions: meals eaten to the sound of the clock, or the father's celery-munching, or the mother's loose false teeth, but not of any real exchange of words or feelings. The mother's false teeth, so tenaciously clung to even on her deathbed, give way in the last stanza to the long gown bought for 'her son's next New York première' as an image of defiant working-class pride.

Yet the affirmative ending effected by this change of focus leaves the problem of silence poignantly unresolved – as it must be. Only such a patched-up finale can adequately suggest the raw edges of unarticulated feeling left bleeding after the lopping off of the parents' lives. Harrison has found a perfect form for the kind of experience – unspoken or half-spoken, puzzled, unruly – that most resists neat aesthetic or intellectual formulation. If T.S. Eliot's great achievement in 'The Love Song of J. Alfred Prufrock' was to make the pseudo-failure of technique an enactment of emotional repression, Harrison has done the same thing in 'Illuminations, III', only for the working class instead of the bourgeoisie.

The issue of how to write verse that does not falsify the parents' language is raised in 'Confessional Poetry', one of the eleven poems added to Part Two in *Selected Poems* (1984). Yet here, where a direct confrontation of the formal problem seems to promise so much, there is a shift of focus that is far less functional to an accurate exploration of the filial dilemma than the one discussed above. Art is often vague or downright deceptive, says stanza 1, so what does it matter if Harrison *père* is made to speak in rhyme or metre? In line 9 we are told that he sometimes spoke in metre anyway. An interlocutory voice now asks why, if there was some capacity for poetry in the father, he is represented as so contemptuous of verse in the immediately preceding poem, 'Book Ends, II' – and why, in the same poem, Harrison himself is so derogatory about his father's attempts at composing an epitaph for the mother ('misspelt, mawkish, stylistically appalling').

84

The answer that is offered by the text is no answer at all, not even a deliberate pseudo-answer that will at least clarify the problem. What Harrison confesses to is only that he and his father fell out, and he is trying to 'make it up' (i.e. both imaginatively re-create the conflict and imaginatively resolve it) by writing a poem about it. To shift attention from the adequacy of representation to the motives behind it is a sleight of hand that leaves the reader with nothing but the most numbing of banalities – namely, that Harrison is a poet for whom poetry is a way of coming to terms with life.

Further – and more successful – attempts at explaining Harrison's motives are 'The Queen's English', 'Aqua Mortis' and 'A Good Read', each of which adds its own persuasive details to the picture of a son obsessed with trying to find words to put in his father's mouth, and with struggling to get inside his father's head. Like a latter-day Faustus who has mortgaged his soul to the pursuit of his art, Harrison now desperately craves the paternal love from which his learning has estranged him: 'My study is your skull. *I'll burn my books*' ('Aqua Mortis'). Even more urgent is the issue of his father's impending death, to avert which an abandonment of books (and more attention to the old man's health?) would be worthwhile. Yet it is the preoccupation with his father's unregenerate otherness that emerges as Harrison's most compelling motive: 'once I'm writing I can't put you down!' Like 'a good read', the father is endlessly fascinating and, once Harrison has begun to address him (as topic and addressee) via the sonnet's insistent formal momentum, there is no way in which (this time, at least) he can subject him to a 'put-down'. A drawback to this eagerness to identify with his father is that it leads Harrison into the sort of compromised position so evident with regard to race in poems like 'Next Door, I and IV'. After exemplifying his adolescent resentment at his father's contempt for reading, Harrison declares:

> I've come round to your position on 'the Arts'
> but put it down in poems, that's the bind.
> (*SP*, p.141)

If this manages not to be quite as arch as 'The Rhubarbarians, II', it is comparably silly. Could the father, who took such a dim view of reading, possibly be said to have a 'position' on the Arts? Could a poet of Harrison's scholarship and craftsmanship seriously represent himself as agreeing with such a position and thinking poetry a 'bind'? Could that same poet truly believe that people like his father would regard sonnets about the father as 'good reads/ for the bus'? There is nothing to redeem such fatuity, especially when it comes from the author of 'Working', 'National Trust' and 'Book Ends, I'. Its worst offence is its bland denial of the very conflict between language and silence which is the thematic lodestone of the whole 'School' sequence. For if the father and people like him can have positions on the Arts that command respect, and if they can read Harrison's own poetry into the bargain, where is the source of all the mutual incomprehension and pain so movingly described elsewhere?

In Chapter 1 (pp. 18–20), I discussed 'The Queen's English' as a particularly good example of Harrison's appropriation of the sonnet form as a vehicle for working-class experience. That poem's subversion of bourgeois hegemonic constraints shows Harrison's ability to carry over into the treatment of family matters the formal victories so tenaciously fought for in more overtly political and historical 'School' sonnets. At the same time, 'A Good Read' should remind us that a hefty slice of demotic bluntness (*'The only score you'd bother with's your darts,/ or fucking football . . .'*) and a comradely arm around the paternal shoulder are not enough by themselves to prise the sonnet free from its incipient élitism and exclusivity: there is no easy compromise to be found between surrendering to the form, ideology included, and actively subverting it. That is not so much a 'bind' as an exacting challenge which Harrison is sometimes not able fully to meet.

Part Three of *Continuous* contains two poems from the first 'School of Eloquence' collection, 'The Earthen Lot' and 't'Ark'. To these are added another eleven poems. *Selected Poems* (1984 and 1987) adds a further four, with 'History Classes' reappearing from the first collection. Although this section lacks the concentrated focus of Parts One and Two, it incorporates a few strikingly successful poems – and none more so than the first one, 'Self Justification'. This addresses the mystery of Harrison's own eloquence by relating it to Uncle Joe's stammering, which prompted him to become a very fast and accurate typesetter. Disability, whether physical or social, is thus a primary motive for self-improvement. The 'aggression, struggle, loss' that Harrison experienced as a working-class boy were simultaneously the obstacles and the incentives to his becoming a poet. His talent is not seen as the bizarrely arbitrary gift which it is in the epigraph-poem 'Heredity'.

Nevertheless, it remains a mystery why, for a few individuals, the inheritance of loss should be such a powerful spur to struggle. To be sure, such a response is fully justified, even if it cannot be adequately explained. The justification is so evident because it could also serve to endorse the collective struggle of working people, in small groups or larger communities and organisations, who have fought to improve their lives against colossal odds. A feeling of radical impoverishment has precipitated some momentous historical struggles, though its precise strength, persistence and consequences have been notoriously difficult to predict. But one further incentive is added to 'aggression, struggle, loss', and that is 'blank printer's ems', the units used to measure the amount of print in a line, page or whole book. In this image the fundamental character of eloquence is acknowledged: it comes about because there is simply a void to be filled, a page to be covered, a silence to be broken. Eloquence in speech, writing or action is existentially necessary to human beings, though some make more use of it than others. In this way Harrison's self-justification reaches back across the familial concerns of Part Two to the wider perspective of Part One.

Another, more explicit return to the idea of collective struggle is 'Dichtung und Wahrheit'. Dedicated to a Frelimo activist, it positions itself alongside the Mozambiquan freedom fighters while rejecting the 'eloquence' of the gun as an ultimate goal for such a struggle. Guns equal power, as Mao's famous saying is invoked to remind us; and what the poem rejects is the pursuit of power at the expense of truth. The Russian word *pravda* neatly encapsulates the systematic abuse of truth, just as the Kalashnikov PK rifle's tongue of flame is a denial of the ends which eloquence should serve. *Dichtung* can speak *Wahrheit* only when the language is a product of human tongues dedicated to humanly redemptive purposes.

Last in the whole sequence comes a group of sonnets entitled 'Art and Extinction', of which 't'Ark' is the culmination. Those that precede it are further variations on the linked themes of language and lost animal species. Poem I asks whether the prodigal use of words will be good or bad for the health of language itself. The answer is that writers – like John James Audubon, who slaughtered birds in order to preserve them in paint – kill the living language by fixing it in print. Compared with the subtle treatment of the extinction theme in 't'Ark', this is much too simplistic. Words may certainly become dog-eared by persistent use, and writers have a constant struggle to 'make it new'; but language (as opposed to languages – and the cultures that support them!) does not die as irrevocably as animals do. There is surely the world of difference between a fossilised metaphor and a stuffed dodo. In any case, words suffer far more from being *under*-used, as poems such as 'Working' and 'The Rhubarbarians, I' so forcibly remind us. Or perhaps we should say that words suffer from being overused only by the wrong people; but the antidote to this can only be more eloquence from the oppressed, not less of it.

'Divisions, I & II' anticipate the more sustained attention to machismo and cultural crisis that occurs in *v*. The skinheads' tattoos, drunkenness and soccer team loyalty are all seen as symptomatic of their economic hopelessness. Their aggression is a familiar male reaction to unemployment. In poem II the stereotype of brown ale-drinking Northern working-class masculinity is subjected to some wry debunking as a pathetic misdirection of the young men's energies. Such crude false consciousness is easy to identify and to challenge. As I argued in Chapter 2, however, Harrison's own self-image owes a good deal to a limiting conception of what it is to be a man, and to a concomitant lack of concern about the fullness of women's experience.

Blake Morrison is entirely justified in including Harrison among those postwar poets who are obsessed with their parents, particularly their fathers.[19] In Harrison's case there is no denying the intensity of that preoccupation: of the twenty-three family poems in Part Two of *Continuous*, well over half (I count fourteen) are primarily about the father, though the mother also figures in several. Only five are focused more on the mother, with a further four that are concerned equally with both parents. A minor redress is achieved in *Selected Poems* (1987), with its additional sonnets about the mother in Part Two: ' "Testing the Reality" ', 'The Effort' (about 'her ferocious pride' and 'tender hands'), 'Bye-Byes' (a mawkish performance, not redeemed by its arch simplicity) and 'Jumper' (about the reassuring rhythm of his mother's wartime knitting). As well as these, there are another three mostly about the father: 'Breaking the Chain' and 'Painkillers, I & II'.

But whatever the latest count, the father–son relationship is too subtle and pervasive to be measured by simple arithmetic; for there is a consistent attempt to understand the father's limitations, and even to make common cause with them, whereas the mother's attitudes (in contrast to her often comforting physical presence) tend to be offered as examples of proletarian female prejudice without much effort to mitigate them, let alone identify any truth they may – however distortedly – contain. 'Bringing Up' shows her as implacably hostile to *The Loiners*, yet there is no reconciling generosity on Harrison's part – no admission that, within the rigid confines of her puritanism, she had a view worthy of sympathy, if not of respect. To his dead father he can say that he has come to agree with him about the Arts: such a gesture towards his mother's no more limited point of view is unthinkable. It strikes me as a real deficiency that the author of 'The Nuptial Torches' and 'Working' should marginalise a woman's experience to this extent, especially when that woman is his mother. (For a fuller discussion of Harrison's gender position, see Chapter 2, pp. 35–41; Chapter 3, pp. 60–6.)

The original group of sonnets that made up *From 'The School of Eloquence' and other poems* were primarily about language as an instrument of power and therefore, inescapably, of political struggle. Under the auspices of Edward Thompson's passionately engaged historiography, Harrison achieved some of his most intelligent and, at the same time, most strongly felt poems. Subsequent extensions of the '*School*' sequence have left the overtly political poems outnumbered by poems which are instead absorbed with the details of family and neighbourhood life. To be sure, a 'later' poem like 'Self Justification' can demonstrate how to match a class perspective with a full recognition of the ineluctable compulsion which creative writing has always been. Nevertheless, the general direction of development in the '*School*' sequence has been away from a committed, socialistic view of his *class*, in all its historical, cultural and personal dimensions, and towards a characteristically liberal concern with individual experience. This change of perspective has produced some moving observations on Harrison's family life; but it has been achieved at some cost. The idea of language, not as private property or the preserve of an élite, but as the means to emancipation for the inarticulate masses: that is a definitive absence in many of the more recent '*School*' poems and it leaves its mark on that brave attempt at social comment, *v.*, which is the subject of the next chapter.

v.: *from Dover Beach to Beeston Hill*

'National unity? Up yours, sunshine.'
(Gethin Price in Trevor Griffiths's *Comedians*)

Two years before the public furore over Tony Harrison's televised reading of *v.* (first broadcast by Channel 4 on November 4th 1987) started, I attended a much less contentious reading of the poem in the basement of a Leeds bookshop across the road from the University. Harrison had brought along his friend Jack Shepherd, who was then acting in *The Mysteries* at the National Theatre. The two of them performed the dialogue in *v.*, with Shepherd impersonating the disaffected skinhead and Harrison taking the 'Harrison'/poet-narrator role. It was the first time I had come across the poem, which had only recently been published; but it was possible, even at a first hearing, to place it in an intelligible relationship to established lines of development in Harrison's work. There was the preoccupation with his estrangement – by education, inspiration, and finally bereavement – from his working-class mother and father. There was his wider concern with working-class experience as a whole, and the trauma of urban-industrial change in particular. There were the dazzling verbal ingenuity and the revitalisation of traditional metrical patterns and rhyme-schemes. It was, in short, a characteristically honest and skilful piece of work. But what also struck me at the time – and what became clearer as I later read and reread the poem – was Harrison's enormous ambition in attempting to say something in poetry about complex and urgent social issues of the day.

As I argue in Chapter 2, Harrison adopted in *The Loiners* a liberationist sexual politics that belonged very much to the 1960s. By the late 1970s his early 'School of Eloquence' sonnets had staked out a moving and authoritative relation to his own family, and to the historical sufferings of his class. Now, with *v.*, he was making an uncompromising intervention in the politics of the mid 1980s. Listening to Shepherd's and Harrison's reading was a challenging experience, first because of the issues addressed; secondly because of the powerful modulations of the 'acted' speech; and thirdly because one could foresee something – though not, by any means, all – of the outrage that would eventually greet the dissemination of the poem to a mass audience.

Just how bilious and superficial that outrage was can be judged from later (Bloodaxe) editions of the poem, in which a selection of reviews and listener responses is provided. All the tabloid vapourings about obscenity were, of course, quite unable to discredit the poem. What they did succeed in doing, however, was to deflect attention away from the relevance of the poem's ideas and on to one dimension only of the competing social voices through which those ideas are expressed. If the poem has any final limitations, they are nothing to do with gratuitous offensiveness but are, instead, a direct and creditable outcome of its willingness to take risks in dramatising a cultural crisis and imagining its solution.

The first (1985) edition of *v.* carries on the back cover a blurb that draws attention to the poem's setting – 'a vandalised cemetery in Leeds during the Miners' Strike' – and indicates two of the probable meanings of the title letter – 'versus' and 'verses'. At the same time, the reference to the Miners' Strike should remind us that social conflicts involve both success and failure, that 'v' can stand for victory, and that the V-sign can be a gesture of defiant confidence as well as one of aggressive rejection. Harrison's choice of an epigraph from a newspaper interview with Arthur Scargill seems to align the poem with the mining communities' resistance to Ian MacGregor's programme of pit closures; but it is Scargill's father's interest in language that is the subject of the quotation: 'My father still reads the dictionary every day. He says your life depends on your power to master words' (*Sunday Times*, 10 January 1982). The 'power' that is referred to is the mastery of language as such: we are not given any of Scargill's comments about how language-mastery might be mobilised on behalf of class, community or social change, objectives to which his own considerable fluency has been unwaveringly (if not always successfully) directed.

It is not difficult to see the appeal of the Scargill quotation for Harrison. First, it testifies to a continuity of commitment from one generation to the next: the relationship between father and son is based on the sort of mutual respect and understanding which were often lacking between Harrison senior and the scholarship boy whose poems were thought 'mucky' by his mother. Secondly, it speaks of an interest in language as passionate and persistent as Harrison's own. This privileging of linguistic and familial issues has its parallel in the poem that follows.

But before I turn directly to these, or to the other issues addressed in the poem, it is important to take a brief look at the politics of its form. Gray's 'Elegy Written in a Country Churchyard' is the chief source of the alternately rhymed (*a b a b*) four-line stanzas; but Harrison rings some remarkable changes on the steady, meditative plod of Gray's lines:

> Next millennium you'll have to search quite hard
> to find my slab behind the family dead,
> butcher, publican, and baker, now me, bard
> adding poetry to their beef, beer and bread.

This is the first stanza, and it declares the poem's historical and ideological distance from Gray with uncompromising directness. The iambic beat, preserved intact in line 2, is elsewhere thoroughly disrupted: line 3 especially is irregular to the point of a quantum difference from anything Gray would have countenanced or been capable of. And the reason for this prosodic GBH is Harrison's paramount need to assert his solidarity with the dead artisans of his own family and class. Where Gray looks on as the detached – though undoubtedly sympathetic – middle-class observer of the hamlet's 'rude Forefathers', Harrison is contemplating his own origins and anticipating his death as a means of being reunited with his ancestors. Where Gray invokes Hampden, Milton and Cromwell to emphasise the gulf between their illustrious public lives and the humble, unsung virtues of the buried rustics, Harrison drives home his insistence on poetry-as-craft/poet-as-artisan by noting the graves of Byron the tanner and Wordsworth the organ-builder (stanzas 2,4).

Yet there are two aspects of Gray's poem which do not need to be radically altered in order to serve Harrison's radical purpose. The 'Elegy' lays great stress on a specific location to which it returns again and again as a stimulus to reflection on more general issues. Substituting an urban cemetery for Gray's rural one, Harrison moves outward in a very similar way from the immediate physical setting to take in history, social conflict and the nature of mortality. Also, the 'Elegy' is the most successful of Gray's attempts to combine his (mostly classical) learning with an accessible style. The simplicity of his syntax and diction can be correctly regarded as a model for Harrison's sombre thoughts, and even for the skinhead's bone-hard, battering locutions.

v. opens with images of vertical and horizontal ancestry. On the vertical axis are the occupants of the cemetery poised above the empty galleries of a long-disused pit. The narrator is positioned horizontally in relation to the community of decent people whose graves lie all around him. Both planes converge in the image of a hypothetical ultimate levelling down that will collapse the graveyard into the 'lowest worked-out seam' of the mine. This idea of the past exerting a geological pressure on the present will recur at the end of the poem, where it will serve as a means of formal closure. At this stage it supplies a crucial image by which vandalism and football hooliganism can be historically and socially situated:

> This graveyard stands above a worked-out pit.
> Subsidence makes the obelisks all list.
> One leaning left's marked FUCK, one right's marked
>   SHIT
> Sprayed by some peeved supporter who was pissed.
>
>   *(SP*, p. 236)

The supporters are 'peeved', not just because of their team's disappointing performance mentioned in the two preceding stanzas; their whole world is skewed and slanted by the worked-out remnants of the industrial past. Even the sturdy obelisk of a prosperous banker is subject to the universal slippage. Worked-out also are the words of the dead generations whose lapidary Latin and religious references have given way to the sprayed obscenities of skinheads.

The 'v' which has been sprayed everywhere in the cemetery provides a compound symbol of many of society's conflicts in 1984, from Football League battles to the larger wars of class, industry, race, religion and gender. In three stanzas the poem supplies a comprehensive list of major national and international problems, then in a fourth concludes:

> The prospects for the present aren't too grand
> when a swastika with NF (National Front)'s
> sprayed on a grave, to which another hand
> has added, in a reddish colour, CUNTS.
>
> (*SP*, p. 238)

The 'not-too-grand' kind of Yorkshire understatement refuses to get over-emotional about life's trials, while at the same time not blinking the awfulness of what is witnessed. The NF swastika and anti-NF obscenity are equally depressing indications of contemporary decline. Both are instances of vandalism, and 'CUNTS' is a typical piece of misogynistic verbal violence. Nevertheless, given the scale of racial hatred in Britain – and Leeds is a serious trouble spot – can 'CUNTS' be quite so easily equated with a swastika? Harrison's indiscriminate pessimism is partly sanctioned by the previous stanza's characterisation of 'Man' as 'resigned/ To hope from his future what his past never found'. Over the next twenty stanzas, recollections of the past and observations of the contemporary scene are punctuated with admissions of guilt and confessions of puzzled impotence. Harrison has spent only an 'odd ten minutes' at his parents' grave since they died. Now he has not got the time to scrub the skinhead's word off their stone, even if he wanted to. Instead it is more productive to concentrate on the ironic aptness of 'UNITED', and wishfully to convert it into

> an accident of meaning to redeem
> an act intended as mere desecration
> and make the thoughtless spraying of his team
> apply to higher things, and to the nation.
>
> (*SP*, p. 240)

Harrison owns up to his wishfulness, but the strategy of imaginative incorporation he has adopted is stretched to breaking point when it is required to cope with the skinhead. Now decent hesitancy

('It isn't all his [the skinhead's] fault though. Much is ours.')
gives way to downright bewilderment:

> Jobless though they are how can these kids,
> even though their team's lost one more game,
> believe that the 'Pakis', 'Niggers', even 'Yids'
> sprayed on the tombstones here should bear the blame?
>
> *(SP*, p. 240)

As part of the poem's incremental structure of enquiry and
argument, this stanza occupies a crucial place. It acknowledges
the vital connection between unemployment, soccer fan subculture
and racism; yet at the same time it testifies to the helplessness felt
by decent people in the face of violent prejudices they cannot
adequately explain, let alone correct. We should register the insufficiency of Harrison's liberal perspective at this point – whether
he was fully aware of it himself or not.

The arrival of the skinhead interlocutor drags the focus of the
poem away from dreams of reconciliation back to recalcitrant social
reality. This is accomplished chiefly by an anti-intellectual tirade
directed against educated language. It is a scorching indictment
of well-meaning ineffectuality; but, like the position of Harrison
himself, it is uncomfortably problematical. For the skinhead is
shown not as a lumpen-proletarian racist but as a tough-minded
class warrior whose venom is reserved solely for the educated middle
class, including the embourgeoised Harrison:

> *Don't talk to me of fucking representing*
> *the class yer were born into any more.*
> *Yer going to get 'urt and start resenting*
> *it's not poetry we need in this class war.*
>
> *(SP*, p. 244)

There is certainly nothing wrong with such an attack. It is simply
that it does not obviously belong in a poem about racism, vandalism
and urban futility. Instead of embodying the endemic fascism of
an unequal society, the skinhead is shown first as the voice of
Harrison's liberal conscience and then as the Janus-face of his

compromised class position. Thus the poem shifts from the larger public arena towards a concern with family loyalty and class betrayal. Our sympathies are enlisted first on behalf of the skinhead's class resentment and then a second time as his whole perspective is taken on board as the hitherto-unacknowledged 'other' of Harrison's liberalism: 'He aerosolled his name. And it was mine.'[1]

Racism does not, however, drop out of sight altogether. The poem goes on to describe the impact of immigration on a working-class neighbourhood and the problems of adjustment this created for Harrison's father. His suspicion and hostility towards Asians are treated sympathetically, but also with careful detachment. A fine balance is obviously required if the father's attitudes are not to be implicitly endorsed:

> House after house FOR SALE where we'd played cricket
> with white roses cut from flour-sacks on our caps,
> with stumps chalked on the coal-grate for our wicket,
> and every one bought now by 'coloured chaps',
>
> dad's most liberal label as he felt
> squeezed by the unfamiliar, and fear
> of foreign food and faces, when he smelt
> curry in the shop where he'd bought beer.
>
> (*SP*, p. 246)

And four stanzas later we are told:

> But when he bought his cigs he'd have a chat,
> his week's one conversation, truth to tell,
> but time also came and put a stop to that
> when old Wattsy got bought out by M. Patel.
>
> (*SP*, p. 247)

The danger here is that Harrison, having silenced the skinhead's racism, might allow it back into the poem by underwriting his father's attitudes. Did 'old Wattsy' really get 'bought out' by M. Patel, with all that that can imply of ruthless commercial and cultural aggrandisement? Or did old Wattsy willingly sell because Mr Patel was offering the best price – maybe the only price? If, for some readers, the tightrope of fairness is not walked without some wobbling here, we are still a long way from Albert Camus's refusal to denounce French colonialism in Algeria because it would have meant condemning his own mother.

Unlike his father, Harrison now has his centre of gravity elsewhere. Towards the end of the poem he returns to his wife and a warm fireside where he can listen to Alban Berg and reflect on the significance of what has happened in the cemetery.[2] Never, until his ashes are buried there, will he go back. This double self-exile – from working-class Leeds as much as from his parents' grave – is sanctioned by an extended meditation on the insignificance of social ills under the aspect of eternity: the 'old violence and old disunity' of 'police v. pickets' at Orgreave or Catholic v. Protestant in Northern Ireland are a mere moment in the span of geological time. Drawing a perspective from 'at least 300 million years ago', when primeval forests began to be converted into the coal seams that lie beneath Beeston Hill Cemetery, the poem is able to endorse the skinhead's 'UNITED' as an unwitting expression of human community:

> I hear [. . .] ghosts from all Leeds matches humming
> with one concerted voice the bride, the bride
> I feel united to, *my* bride is coming
> into the bedroom, naked, to my side.
>
> The ones we choose to love become our anchor
> when the hawser of the blood-tie's hacked, or frays.
> But a voice that scorns chorales is yelling: *Wanker!*
> It's the aerosolling skin I met today's.
>
> My *alter ego* wouldn't want to know it,
> his aerosol vocab would baulk at LOVE,
> the skin's UNITED underwrites the poet,
> the measures carved below the ones above.
>
> I doubt if 30 years of bleak Leeds weather
> and 30 falls of apple and of may
> will erode the UNITED binding us together.
> And now it's your decision: does it stay?
>
> (*SP*, pp. 248–9)

Although the final decision about the aptness of 'UNITED' is left to posterity, there are still some questions to be asked right now. What kind of 'unity' is at issue here, after all? Is it any more than the last-ditch mutual loyalty that provides Matthew Arnold's only source of comfort at the end of 'Dover Beach' ('Ah, love, let us be true/ To one another!')? Harrison is surely attempting to encompass something more than romantic love. Whereas Arnold uses the elemental imagery in 'Dover Beach' to represent all that threatens personal 'love . . . light . . . certitude', and so on, Harrison invokes geomorphology as a global and timeless process which, by affecting us all, can be regarded as a species of unifying destiny. The only final victory belongs to 'vast, slow, coal-creating forces/ that hew the body's seams to get the soul'.

Yet there remains the awkward short-term problem of Harrison's relationship to all that the skinhead represents as spokesman for Northern working-class disaffection – that is to say, his relationship to society and history as opposed to geology and eternity. Here the poem's formal closure is most ingenious, for the skinhead and Harrison are united in being equally subject to geological forces. More subtly still, they are the surface and substratum of human community itself. The skinhead's 'UNITED' is the transient expression (it can be rubbed off the gravestone) of a unity more permanently 'carved' in the poet's 'measures' underneath. However, we have been told that the skinhead is Harrison's other self and, as such, it is not easy to accept him now as a mere surface that superficially denies, but unwittingly confirms, Harrison's optimism about social unity. In the last two stanzas we are also told that Harrison's chiselled epitaph must be read with one's 'back to Leeds'. That awkward relationship to contemporary urban life cannot be reversed by the epitaph's acknowledgement of 'pit . . . SHIT . . . beef . . . beer . . . bread' as the material reality out of which the poem has grown. What it does do, however, is measure the distance that separates Harrison's engagement with the realities of work and culture from those of Matthew Arnold a hundred years before. The scholarship boy knows about social deprivation and conflict from the perspective of the oppressed; Arnold's view, for all its liberal concern, was inescapably that of the oppressors.

By far the largest photograph in the first Bloodaxe edition of *v.* (and a smaller, grainier, close-up version of it is repeated further on) spreads across the two title-pages and shows a young man outside Leeds United football ground reaching into his back pocket for the money to buy a racist newspaper from a member of the National Front. (This photograph appears on page 14 of the second edition.) Two mounted policemen are busily (or indifferently?) watching the football crowd disperse, paying no attention at all to the racist propaganda that is being peddled within a few feet of them. It is a potent image of the relationship between the forces of law and order and certain kinds of organised violence in 1980s Britain. If we recall how the police were deployed against miners during the 1984/5 Strike, the photograph is doubly disturbing. It says a lot about the scale of Tony Harrison's ambition in tackling, at that precise time, explosive issues like race, class and unemployment. If he dramatises social tensions so potent that he cannot finally domesticate them to a humane optimism about the future, this does not detract from the ingenuity and courage with which he has addressed them.

In a BBC 'Omnibus' interview in September 1991, the American novelist Don DeLillo offered a rationale for writers like himself continuing to grapple with the 'turmoil' of 'contemporary life'. His plea to Western societies beset by apparently intractable problems was: 'If we can't find a solution, let's imagine one' – which is precisely where writers enter the frame. The snag is that imagining solutions (to reverse the formula) can become a substitute for trying to find them. Harrison's dream of ultimate social unity in *v.* could have been such a diversion from the puzzling, painful business of social betterment in cities like Leeds. 'Could have been', because the great achievement of the poem is finally in allowing its own dialectic – its commitment to the 'versus' principle, no matter where it leads – to provide the means by which its attempted closure can be deconstructed. In his other political interventions Harrison often combines conflicting elements of liberalism and socialism, wishful thinking and shrewd analysis, despair and hope. At the same time, with his back to Leeds or not, Harrison's view from Beeston Hill never entirely overlooks either the individual or the collective features of contemporary life.

The American poems

Poetry never stood a chance
of standing outside history.
(Adrienne Rich, 'North American Time')

Between the last of the 'School of Eloquence' sonnets and the first
of the poems set in America there is one poem, 'Facing North'
(*SP*, pp. 190–91). The poem's epigraph from Louis MacNeice
emphasises Northernness as a state of mind and feeling, rather
than a simple physical origin or location: 'The North begins inside.'
In the meditation/lucubration that follows, the 'North' is extended
beyond its typical English associations – of dourness, ugliness,
lack of compromise – to encompass an older, more archetypal
image of all that has immemorially threatened human comfort,
not to say complacency. 'The whole view North', with its darker
and darker perspective on both past and present, is an essential
element in Harrison's vision. His continuing exposure to that
chilling but bracing challenge reinforces his artistic survival skills
('elbow grease,/ deep thought, long practice and much sweat').
The unlit, draughty writing-room (presumably in Newcastle) which
Harrison is 'leaving' at the end of the poem is a metonymy for his
continuing – intermittent but unbreakable – commitment to facing the
puzzlement and anguish by which humanity has always been beset.

First of the American poems in *Selected Poems* is 'A Kumquat
for John Keats'. The thirty-two line sentence which opens this
poem unrolls luxuriously, as though Harrison is stretching himself
after hours in a cramped and cold position. What in 'Facing North'
was a beleaguered room surrounded and penetrated by darkness is
now transformed into the fruit whose tart skin and sweet inside
exemplify 'how days have darkness round them like a rind,/ life
has a skin of death that keeps its zest'. Where 'Facing North' was

a poem of darkness and cold wind, 'A Kumquat' is ablaze with light and still heat. Nevertheless, the signs of a predatory and destructive world have not disappeared: Harrison's previous unhappiness, as husband and father, and the constant threat of nuclear annihilation ('a thing no bigger than an urn explodes/ and ravishes all silence, and all odes') are strongly present.

Above all, the last short stanza is a very deliberate reminder of forces that threaten the Edenic fruitfulness and ease of Micanopy, Florida. Buzzards and farmers' saws make a discomforting pendant to the idyll of new-found emotional peace. Although there is a gesture towards a closure in which the 'sourness' of the birds and jagged implements is balanced and made bearable by the 'fresh thermals' and the 'bedsprings' (a reminder of the previous night's lovemaking), they remain awkwardly unassimilated: even the farmer's name, Mr Fowler, introduces the idea of human beings preying on birds, just as buzzards prey on other creatures. A kumquat-like reconciliation of death and life is at least challenged, if not subverted, by Harrison's refusal to end the poem at the carefully poised well-being of 'Fine, for 42!'. Yet this is precisely the point at which some commentators break off (e.g. Douglas Dunn, *Astley*, p. 215; Maureen Duffy, *Astley*, p. 340), as though to sidestep the last six lines altogether. Mary Garofalakis (*Astley*, p. 333) goes one better: she acknowledges the 'bleak cries' of the buzzards, but stops short at the 'comforting memory' of the bedsprings, instead of going on to say that Mr Fowler and his saws are the poem's final image.

In the next poem, 'Skywriting', Harrison is at his desk, but not looking North from Northern England. Like the surface of a swimming pool painted by David Hockney (the poem's dedicatee), Harrison's glass desk-top reflects both the activities across the street ('ballet school,/ meditation group, karate class') and a section of the sky across which aeroplanes have written the word HAPPY. The Californian skywriting recalls the Pasadena New Year Rose Parade, a huge procession of elaborate floral floats that gives Harrison scope for a verbal flowershow of his own:

> A woodwardia howdah delicately sways
> with jonquil rajahs turbaned with bouquets,
> the Cross in crocus and in baby's breath
> but no carnation Christ clamped to his death,

no battered nailheads of black onion seeds,
no spearthrust of poinsettia that bleeds.
A larkspur 'Swoonatra' in lunaria marquee
croons blue dendrobiums as do-re-mi,
a eucalyptus Calliope plays
furze and broom ta-ra-ra-boom-de-ays.

(SP, p. 196)

This is a dazzling display of Harrison's linguistic range. The second line alone crams together words of Anglo-Saxon, Latin, Hindi, Turkish and French origin. The last four lines play off the scientific, Latinate/Greek precision of the flower names against pop-cultural lingo and the tonic sol-fa. The whole concoction is a brilliant verbal equivalent to the vulgarly energetic, freewheeling omnivorousness of the pageant's inspiration. But the pageant is reduced to wilt and rot the next day. The attempt to fashion optimism out of such perishable materials is doomed to failure, at least for the now gloomy poet seeing it all reflected in his desk:

Life made out of minutes rings as true
as floragraphs of Cherokee and Sioux,
and like igloos quilted out of eglantine
1980's made from '79!

(SP, p. 197)

The real continuity here is not that of 'true' happiness but of the chronic attempt to make a viable collective life out of fragmentation dressed up as art – Disneyland as destiny. Now the poet's desk reflects a night sky dark as a pit. Gradually even the stars are extinguished, and he is left with an 'abyss' whose blackness is intensified by the 'self-help' classes and determined merrymaking going on outside. Like the black-faced Turkish Knight ('In comes I'), he is the one who stands opposed to the relentless optimism of the other 'mummers'; 'tarred' by the blackness of his own ink (creativity; bleakness of vision), the poet is like Banquo's ghost ceaselessly insisting that 'The Pasadena HAPPY turns to cloud!' It is his, and other writers', role to go on 'repeating the same cry/ until the seas of ink have all run dry'.

The Disneyfication of reality is the theme of 'The Call of Nature'. Just as the rubbernecking sightseers to New Mexico try to exclude the hot-dog stall from their carefully composed photographs, so the whole history of the Pueblo Indians is falsified and their current existence impoverished by the movie-extra roles that are their only source of work. D.H. Lawrence, the fiftieth anniversary of whose death the poem commemorates, is no more than 'the priest of sex' to the sightseers who visit Taos, where he lived. They do not even bother to get off the tourist bus, but sit and 'smell the pine/ not spritzed from aerosols but genuine'. The rhyming of 'pine' and 'genuine' fixes the Southwestern USA location and simultaneously invokes a powerful (and, for the English, stereotypical) image of gum-chewing philistinism. The only 'call of nature' the tourists respond to is the need to go to the lavatory; and the 'Braves' and 'Squaws' into which they are separated by the coyly named entrances to their respective toilets is a devastating final swipe at the way that tourism trivialises both gender relations and the fate of indigenous American culture.

'Oh, Moon of Mahagonny' (originally the last of the *U.S. Martial* sequence; see pp. 45–6 above) and 'The Red Lights of Plenty' take the exposure of American crassness back into the city – New York first, then Washington. Central to 'Oh, Moon' is the irony of the Rockefeller family's providing a soirée for the cast of a production of Brecht and Weill's *Mahagonny*. The play is a satire (from 1929) on well-heeled hedonism, the destruction of which, according to the principles of dialectical materialism, is confidently predicted. Harrison ruefully testifies to the enduring power of capitalism, its ability to divert concern about politics and social justice away from the major issue of America's own exorbitant wealth *vis-à-vis* the rest of the world and on to conscience-salving gestures such as 'which caviar to boycott first!'. The idea that the rich might be excluded from the Kingdom of Heaven is as incomprehensible to the New York glitterati as the proposition that the PanAm flights from JFK might cease to take off regularly. Marc Chagall, decorator of the Metropolitan Opera House foyer, is invoked at the end of the poem only to be told that his special brand of dream-imagery would be more appropriately employed, were he to do the whole job again, in depicting 'bread and circuses, lame Pegasi/ and camels that hoopla through the needle's eye!' What for Brecht were the foredoomed contradictions of capitalism have become the entrenched topsy-turvydom of art even – revolutionary art, like Brecht's – served up as one more expensive dish for the conspicuous consumption of thoughtless pleasure-seekers.

'The Red Lights of Plenty' commemorates the centenary of Karl Marx's death in 1883. Set in Washington, the political and military centre of the world's most powerful capitalist nation, it exposes the terminal destructiveness of rampant materialism. 'Plenty' in the New World is not the 'still half benign' largesse of the mythical cornucopia figured in stone 'next to the Law Court's Fallout Shelter'.[1] On the contrary, it is better represented by *The American Wrecking Co.* smashing down a still-modern and structurally sound building to make room for more 'enterprises'. A pumpkin, potent image of moral endurance and hard work rewarded, rots on a porch, its 'gouged eyes' contemplating the 'glare' of World War Three, while a young Black is chased and arrested, and red lights revolve in the darkness.

As in Robert Lowell's 'For the Union Dead', modern urban America is being shaken to pieces by the violence of its own greed and inequalities. Autumn, which should bring an abundant harvest for everyone, becomes a terminal Fall that will engulf the world in the same way as the leaves are sucked up by the vacuum cleaners that maintain the White House's well-manicured image. The 'Hoovering' that takes place in the final line is a sardonic reference to both Herbert and J. Edgar Hoover – the first of whom presided over the previous most irresponsible phase of American capitalism, while the second was the infamously autocratic and vindictive head of the FBI. Thus America's wanton materialism and the repressive state apparatus that supports it are neatly dovetailed into a single devastating image.

Another pair of poems with a great deal in common is 'The Lords of Life' and 'The Fire-Gap'. The first has a title taken from D.H. Lawrence's 'Snake' where the creature is described as 'one of the lords of life' at the end of the poem. Here Harrison's nature-loving, contemplative attitudes are posed against the redneck machismo of his snake-squashing, alligator-shooting Florida neighbour. It is an opposition as complete as any in the Harrison canon. There is no discovery here (as in *v.*) that the antagonist is also a part of the poet's own character, or at least a version of what the poet might have become. Even the beer-drinking would-be camaraderie of the 'cracker neighbour' only emphasises the huge gulf that separates him from the poet, whom he sees as at best eccentric and at worst a 'fairy'.

What the poem establishes most forcibly is not the predictable differences of temperament between the two men, but the terrifying continuity that links the American obsession with guns to rampant nationalism and the Kennedy assassination. Only the space rockets launched from Cape Canaveral (for a short time renamed Cape Kennedy) are exempt from the condemnation of technology-as-violence: they are compared with the black-and-white snake admired by Harrison and brutally beaten to death by his neighbour. At the end of the poem we are left with the ultimate irreconcilability of the snake/rocket's graceful efficiency with the self-destructive brutality of the 'giant gator hunter killing BUD!'. The 'Bud' here is both the canned Budweiser beer guzzled in huge quantities and the 'buddies' – fellow-males – who can easily become targets for the false frontiersmanship of contemporary America.

Mary Garofalakis finds Harrison too 'tolerant', too much the 'contemplater', to 'stand up, and fight for a cause' in this poem (*Astley*, p. 333). According to her, 'the "BUD"(dy) which ends the poem is more significant than the "killing" for the poet who is "feeling too composed to break the spell"' (*ibid.*, p. 334). This is wrong. Harrison may not feel able or willing to challenge the neighbour directly, but the poem itself is far from being quietistic or resigned in its response to what the neighbour represents. After 'feeling too composed' to stop a mosquito gently sucking his blood, Harrison asserts his 'doer side' and 'swats the bastard'. Thus he graphically contradicts the neighbour's view of him and shows that his tolerance is not to be confused with fear, indifference or blinkered optimism.

In 'The Fire-Gap' the snake is not the harmless oaksnake of 'The Lords of Life' but a deadly diamondback rattler. It therefore exemplifies more strikingly (pun intended) the co-presence of beauty and danger, 'Darkness and Light', life and death. Its six-foot length can span the fire-gap between wilderness (its natural home) and the cultivated land on Harrison's property. Despite its fearsome reputation ('this laithliest of laithly worms') and his redneck neighbour's' eagerness to kill it, Harrison wants it to stay, though he is scared of confronting it one day as he walks along the fire-gap to his shed-study. The risk he takes each day in checking the gopher-hole for the rattler's presence is a necessary aspect of his awed excitement at the idea of the snake. Nothing short of being attacked by it will persuade Harrison to add this snake to the tally of those he once killed in Africa and Brazil. For to him, as to Lawrence, the snake mysteriously embodies the wholeness and continuity of life. Such is his respect for the creature that at one point he reverses their positions and pleads with the snake to be allowed to pass 'unmolested', so that he can continue to try to learn what the 'Earth-lover' snake 'already know[s]'.

Yet the snake is continually at risk from the 'Bible-belters' who regard all snakes as the archetypal Serpent, on a par with those other devils in their demonology, 'the fairy, pacifist, the Red/ maybe somebody who loves the Muse'. The twin tails (or forked tongue?) of the poem's ending offer two equally plausible conclusions: the first emphasising (like 'The Lords of Life') the direct link between religious bigotry and aggressive nationalism; the second privileging the tail-swallowing snake and the tale-telling poet as twin symbols of a 'real eternity' more natural and more creative than the miserably punitive universe invoked by the zealots.

There is a third obvious pairing of poems: 'Following Pine' and 'Cypress and Cedar'. Both focus steadily on different kinds of wood, organising their respective smells and uses into metaphors for personal and public realities and the complex interactions between the two. 'Following Pine' is a long narrative poem in three sections that follows the movements and thoughts of Harrison and his wife, Teresa Stratas, through a single day spent going to buy, transporting home and finally planting out non-coniferous saplings in defiance of the uniform pine forests all around their land. Their choice of trees to plant is richly suggestive, 'fig-trees, vines, and apples' (later a pear is also mentioned), each drawing into the poem associations of fecundity, resilience, pleasurable indulgence and hard-won knowledge. The motorway journey by which the trees are brought back is a nightmare of wet road, dead animals on the verges, and heavy traffic. Unfortunately, this section of the poem (stanzas 6–14) is too long: the accumulating details are dwelt on with wearisome precision, so that the accurate sense of a long, frustrating and at times dangerous journey is allowed to be blurred by the tedium of overinsistence and such portentous whimsicality as (apropos the suicidal love-bugs splattered on the car's windscreen) 'Is it just the crushed canoodling gnat/ that needs for its Nirvana nothingness?' The idea of an orgasmic extinction is scrupulously picked up later; but that subsequent use (as a trope for nuclear annihilation) is too clodhoppingly signalled here.

The 'pine-loaded lumber truck' behind which the couple get stuck provides an explanation of the poem's title and a leitmotiv that links such disparate details of American life as the smell of newly built houses, commercial bathroom spray (to mask the smell of reality), Thoreau's Walden Pond experiment in living close to nature, and the Cold War mania for building underground nuclear survival shelters. In the grim light of the latter phenomenon, the couple's determination to plant trees 'with life-spans more than three times yours and mine' is a gesture of unquenchable optimism. But such hope for the future, like that of the *'fourmi'*, will be no better than living only for the present, like the *'cigale'*, if the human race itself is wiped out. The best survival technique of all would be not the delusive skills of hunting and living rough, but the passionate pursuit of knowledge which would always rather learn more about the world than diminish by a fraction its wonderful variety. Harrison's own delighted discovery of the names of woodland trees ('persimmon . . . possumhaw') is related to Socrates's hunger for knowledge even in the face of his impending death. That alliance between tree-planting poet and martyred philosopher completes the first and longest of the poem's three sections.

Section II opens with a contrast between the sterility of the Moon and the Earth's 'warm dirt'. This provides the controlling metaphor(s) for what follows. The light 'beamed off that dead land' enables Harrison and Stratas to plant their trees and thus affirm their commitment to the future – *a* future. The Moon then represents the possible (non)future of a sterile post-Holocaust Earth, *in the light of which* the couple make their hopeful gesture. It takes just over half this section (five stanzas out of nine) to establish this connection; the rest of the section is given over to microscopic observation/speculation about insect and spider behaviour in relation to their probable takeover of a nuclear-polluted planet. As in Section I, there is a self-indulgent trawling of minutiae that collapses into whimsicality – so much so that the final line ('Let's forget about the world until we wake!') looks almost flippant in its loudly understated stoicism.

Section III opens with 'insect movements' and a spider's web (stanza 1), then abruptly shifts to the couple meeting naked in the early morning to water their saplings. Breaking through the 'net' of spider filaments, associated with entrammelment in the 'stricture[s]' of fatalism and unfreedom, Harrison strides forward to be united with his wife. However, there are pine needles and possible rattlesnakes underfoot, so he must tread warily even as he moves doggedly towards 'the world of day'. The final paradox of the couple's situation is that their love for each other, and their early-morning nakedness, would be more screened and safeguarded from the world if they were 'enclosed with pine'; yet that phrase strongly suggests a coffin and a death-like withdrawal from reality. The fact that they have not opted for a quick-growing defence against the world, but have wagered so completely on openness, risk and a belief in the long-term (i.e. slow-growing) future, is a final persuasive tribute to a love that will not deny its roots in a common earth. (The helium-filled mammoth that figures Harrison's sense of growth and aspiration in 'Giving Thanks' is, at the same time, anchored to the ground by nets. Only orgasm gives Harrison a brief, blissful release from all that otherwise keeps his feet on the ground.)

The inescapability of history and social reality; the necessity of art and hope: both are figured in 'Cypress and Cedar' as the balanced opposition of stinking cypress and sweetly aromatic cedar. Throughout this poem the stanza form, *a b c c b a*, pictures the mirror-image reversal of the two woods. The scent of cedar can survive burial (as a fencepost) in the ground. It also permeates and binds together other fragrances, 'damp denim, genitals, "genuine hide leather"', associated with work and sexuality. Its aphrodisiac properties might even have been enough (Harrison speculates) to help Phèdre seduce Hippolyte, leaving Racine with no tragedy to write about. Given that, and its efficacy as a sweetener of everything from cat litter to the tombs of Pharaohs, Harrison asks himself why he bought a chair for himself made of cypress instead of cedarwood like his wife's.

The answer is that cypress has the reek of ancestral origins about it; it is a permanent reminder of the primeval 'stew' from which the human race emerged. It is also especially apt for Harrison's Florida swampland home, named 'Micanopy' by an earlier 'English classicist' with a grim sense of humour, whose descent into 'misery' was unrelieved by marriage and the sweet smells that Harrison enjoys from his wife's cedar clothes chest. Reminders (cypress-like) of ugliness and suffering are everywhere, so that peace of mind can never be more than 'floating' on the 'swamps of pain'.

Floating/drowning, light/darkness, head/heart are the antinomies that embody the eternal struggle to make something humanly bearable out of our links to a perishable world. But within that predicament the pairing of female (cedar) and male (cypress) can offer an intimate complementarity, even exchange, of characteristics. In the same way, if cypress more aptly represents the stink of mortality, art can achieve a clarity and order akin to the cedar-smell that comes from Harrison's pencil in the poem's last line.

So art offers – as it did so powerfully for Keats – some compensation for death and decay as a shared human destiny; but this raises a further problem which Harrison addresses in 'The Heartless Art'. If poetry achieves its consoling shapeliness and durability by the unremitting exercise of technique ('engineering', l. 30), is there a danger that it will not prove equal to the brute truth of a friend-and-neighbour's tragic early death? In other words, are there some intensely personal, intensely painful kinds of experience that must be falsified to some extent by being treated as occasions for the display of virtuosity?

Harrison's rueful admission of defeat, in 'Book Ends, II', when faced with the task of inventing something better than his father's 'stylistically appalling' inscription for his mother's headstone, now finds an answering confidence in this audaciously self-de(con)structing poem. It begins with Harrison outside his neighbour's house, busy protecting kumquat trees against winter frost, but conscious all the time of Seth's terminal illness taking its inevitable course. The adequacy of poetry to describe or define what Seth is suffering is challenged (in stanzas 3 and 4) via a piece of shop-talk in which Harrison confesses to breaking up the word Methadone ('Meth/a-done') in order to make a rhyme for death; yet such ingenuity, partially justified by Seth's own breathless articulation of the drug-name, still falls short of 'just saying' that he 'fought for breath', which would have involved a repetition of the 'breath' at the end of a previous line. Harrison admits (in stanza 5) that the 'Meth-death' rhyme was also to avoid his having to use a different 'death' rhyme which – always the poet – he had 'stowed away' the first time he met Seth Tooke and realised that he was terminally ill. Stanza 6 ends with Harrison's defiant completion of that stored rhyme '[death-] SETH'.

Next, Harrison offers to distract Seth from his pain by showing him 'a bit about my metre, line and rhyme'. This he proceeds to do by explaining why he would not (like Arthur Symons) stress 'Nazareth' on its last syllable in order to make it a strong rhyme with 'Death', and thus underline a contrast between death and the prospect of Heaven embodied in Jesus. Harrison affirms that his art is ultimately at the service of his convictions (atheism in this case), as Symons's were. Yet the poet must still admit to a 'final failure', because the poem he mostly wrote a week before Seth's death could not be shown to him. The dying are already highly sensitised to what they see as the condescension of the 'non-dying' (stanza 9): given that, it was better not to bother Seth with poetry at all, let alone a poem that could be completed only by his own demise, the details of which are added at the foot of the poem to be inserted in the parenthetical gaps provided in stanza 10. Harrison asks:

> When I began these lines could I have known
> that the nurse's registration of the time
> you let your spirit go with one last groan
> would help complete the first and third line rhyme?
>
> (*SP*, p. 208)

The rhyme is 'alive–10.05', but its falling neatly into the stanza's rhyme-scheme is not life arbitrarily endorsing art: it is the product of sheer chance and the poet's careful craft. After all, the first insert ('how you stayed alive') was the poet's choice and in no way contingent upon the precise day and time of Seth's death. What looks like a 'failure' at first glance – something that only life/death can validate or correct – turns out to be a modest tribute to the resourcefulness with which poetry can address its own limitations.

Harrison's American poems have been usefully discussed by Mary Garofalakis as 'versus/verses' in which

> every issue is seen as having two different sides – sometimes oppositional but often with the gap between the two filled in such a way that the relationship is one of harmony and/or nurturance. . . . Even though the dualities are not always clearly in conflicting positions, they still retain their differences and most often the poet leaves the question of

the relationship up to the partner/reader to whom the poem is addressed.

(Astley, p. 331)

This is correct in its emphasis on duality, although I do not agree with all Garofalakis's readings of individual poems (see my discussions of 'A Kumquat for John Keats' and 'The Lords of Life' above), nor do I think that Harrison leaves much for the reader to decide (as opposed to agree/disagree with): the weight of emphasis between positive and negative forces is invariably clear for all to see, even – or, rather, especially – where there is an equipoise between the two. In any case, most of the American poems do not just contain crucial dichotomies within themselves; they also offer huge scope for the sort of pairings that I have suggested above. There is a dialectic at work throughout the whole group in which figures of difference confront each other, not (usually) in aid of some narrowly rhetorical resolution nor the cop-out of leaving it up to the reader, but in order to register, as poetry must ceaselessly do, both the complementary and conflictual nature of the existential reality which poetry and love inescapably inhabit.

POSTSCRIPT: 'THE MOTHER OF THE MUSES'

Closely related to the strictly American poems is 'The Mother of the Muses', written to commemorate Teresa Stratas's father, Emmanuel, who died in a Toronto old people's home in 1987. First published in *The London Review of Books*, this poem has been reprinted in a limited private edition by the Rampant Lions Press, then in *Astley's* Bloodaxe anthology and, most recently, in *The Gaze of the Gorgon* (1992), also a Bloodaxe book (see Chapter 7 below). Its dominant theme is memory, a faculty made suddenly precious by the painful spectacle of Emmanuel Stratas and his fellow-'Rest Home denizens' lost in the mental fog of their respective strokes and senility.

Harrison begins the poem with his own struggle to remember a speech from Aeschylus's *Prometheus Bound* that he had once seen scratched, as an ancient *aide-mémoire*, on a fragment of pottery in a museum. But the effort of recollection shifts to the previous day's visit to the 'Home for the Aged almost glazed with ice/ and

111

surrounded by obliterating snow'. Snow stands for everything – ageing, disease, death – that blots out, or smoothes to featurelessness, the landscape of the mind. (Another potential destroyer of memory is fire, that good-and-bad Promethean gift which could consume the Earth in a terminal nuclear blaze.)

As his own assertion of the power of memory against oblivion, Harrison forces himself to recall a series of residents in addition to Emmanuel himself. Elsie, Lilian, Anne, Gene, Joan and Jock: the names are vital, for they affirm a continuing human identity in the midst of humiliating disabilities. Only the pathetic, shrunken woman 'weeping for death in her 92nd year' has gone beyond the point where names – her own or other people's – convey any meaning at all. For the others, fragmentary images and aphasic hesitations measure the attenuation of their links with life: their histories have brought them back to their origins, and this has meant – for those born, like Emmanuel, in non-English-speaking countries – a return to their native speech, and further isolation from everyone else.

In stanza 21 the question is asked:

> If we *are* what we remember, what are they
> who don't have memories as we have ours . . . ?

to which the answer is offered:

> The troubled conscience, though, 's glad to forget.
> Oblivion for some's an inner balm.
> They've found some peace of mind, not total yet,
> as only death itself brings that much calm.
>
> (*GG*, p. 42)

This is only a partial answer. It refers to those among the old for whom forgetting is a relief; and, to confirm this judgement, the next eight stanzas describe vivid memories of the fire-bombing of Dresden recalled by eyewitnesses, and supported by original film footage, in a documentary on the Home's television set. Harrison admits to feeling glad that the old people did not understand the meaning of the horrific stories; but he goes on also to admit that their lack of understanding prevented their appreciating the achievement of the people of Dresden in restoring their opera house (ironically named 'Semper', the Latin word for 'always') to its prewar glory. Such a restoration, involving considerable scientific research, was a colossal act of collective remembering, a willed recovery of cultural riches from virtual obliteration. In contrast to this creative use of memory, another television documentary deals with a man misremembering Germany's Nazi past in order to deny genocide against the Jews. His 'doctoring' of history is supported by some people, 'not just Germans', who cannot maintain their faith in human progress if they accept that the Holocaust happened.

Refusing to be confined for a night to the Home, Harrison and his wife preferred to face the blizzard conditions and drive back. Next day, Harrison resolves to 'make . . . known', as an affirmation of life, his love for/lovemaking with his wife. In the process of declaring this resolution, he echoes a phrase – 'that long thing where you lie' – used the day before by Lilian as she struggled to recall the word coffin. Thus a confused image of death is converted into a sombre, but joltingly precise, figure for the constraints of life and death which the couple's mutual devotion helps them face up to.

In a newspaper review (*The Guardian*, 27 October 1992), Peter Forbes praises the poem's use of 'repetition and prolixity' as 'organic to the subject'. This is an accurate judgement of the poem's structure and purpose; all its accumulated evidence, however fragmentary, is warranted by its insistence on remembering as a permanent struggle against terminal decline. Prometheus (whose name means 'forethought') can be unbound only with the help of Mnemosyne, the mother of all creative endeavour and thus of civilisation itself. The primacy of memory is further explored in Harrison's 1993 film-poem *Black Daisies for the Bride* (see pp. 134–5 below), in which he tries to discover – and, where possible, celebrate – what remains of a person's mental stock, especially an almost ineradicable sense of rhythm, even in the advanced stages of Alzheimer's Disease.

'The Blasphemers' Banquet' and other interventions

'You think the truth is *beautiful*? You've forgotten
what it's *like*.'
(Gethin Price in Trevor Griffiths's *Comedians*)

The frankly interventionist contemporary social commentary in-
augurated by *v.* was closely followed by a collection of seven sonnets
in the 'School of Eloquence' manner published by the aptly named
Scargill Press. Their collective title, *Anno Forty Two*, refers to
the publication date (scrupulously recorded) of 6 August 1987,
forty-two years to the day after the dropping of the Hiroshima atom
bomb. The first five poems are grounded in Harrison's childhood
memories; the last two rely heavily on recondite zoological and
geographical knowledge; but all seven fulfil, to a greater or lesser
degree, the promise of their collective title by dealing with the past
and (possible) future horrors of nuclear war. At the beginning of
the series, 'Old Soldiers' (also in *SP*, p. 159) measures the change
of consciousness wrought by Hiroshima in terms of Harrison's own
irrevocably altered view of that still familiar commercial image,
the 'Camp' coffee label. The two soldiers shown on the label, a
kilted white officer and a Sikh chuprassie, embodied for the young
Harrison the hierarchy and moral stability of an older imperial
order. Through an infinite regression of images ('the label in the
label in the label') the two men were fixed in their immutable
roles – until Hiroshima. The repercussions of that event set a divide
between the child's naive confidence that the old order was 'forever'
and the grown man's knowledge that he can never recover his
younger self's belief in permanence: the image of the eternally
loyal chuprassie is now as empty as the bottle itself, its 'essence'
definitively consumed.

The second, third and fourth sonnets in the sequence are closely linked by their use of photography. 'The Figure' develops a sinister image of death ('the biped draped in black') and of nuclear test explosions ('the tripod') out of the seaside photographer and his old-fashioned equipment. But the figure referred to in the title is that ubiquitous partner of the photographer discernible in the background of 'every family's South Pier snap' from Blackpool in the 1940s and 1950s. He it is, 'in the same frayed suit', who directs the happy-go-lucky family towards the camera and – in his implied aspect of seedy politician – also towards the 'sun' of the first H-bomb explosion the following year (1952).

'Black & White' weaves a complicated opening pattern out of flash photography, the nuclear flash that brought victory against Japan in 1945 and the irony of that defeat's having led to a postwar Japanese boom, one of the benefits of which has been cheaper, better cameras and photographic film. Subsequent images muddy the water considerably as we move from 'sitting ducks', via Captain Hook and Peter Pan, to the blast victim scorched to a silhouette on a Hiroshima wall. The transition from stanza 1 to that final image is so laboured in its metaphorical connections and (in stanza 3) its syntax that the impact of the last line is seriously weakened. A similar enfeeblement afflicts 'Snap', the first half of which is anchored firmly in an image (again photographic) of the Harrison family and others celebrating VJ Day. In the second half a succession of images ('Kirby Wire . . . Jehovaspeak . . . Pentecost') fails to establish a coherent or compelling transition to the final 'Ban the Bomb!'. One is left with two equally unsatisfactory meanings: (i) the 'Apostles' are the original followers of Jesus whose message of peace is translated into the idiom of CND; (ii) the 'Apostles' are the postwar peace campaigners themselves (with an awkward glance at the Cambridge Apostles) who spread the anti-Bomb slogan around the world. Neither meaning is an alternative to the other; but, separately or together, they rely on parallels between first-century Christianity and the modern Peace Movement which are at best tenuous and at worst ludicrous.

A much more consistent performance is 'First Aid in English', in which Harrison's ingenious parodying of his first school English Language textbook is kept convincingly in key with his attack on totalitarianism, genocide and the Bomb. Each of the four stanzas contributes its share to the progressive elaboration of the 'collective noun' motif, while the typical textbook exercise proves an eerily appropriate analogy for the final (nuclear) test which no one will pass:

> Cats in their clowder, lions in their pride,
> but there's no aid in English, first or last,
> for a [Fill in the Blank . . .] of genocide
> or more than one [Please Tick . . .] atomic blast.
>
> (*GG*, p. 15)

Peter Forbes has complained that the image of 'burning birds in military conflagrations' occurs so often in Harrison's work that 'it takes on more of a private significance and less of the symbolic quality the poet intended' (*The Guardian*, 27 October, 1992). This image is certainly prominent in 'The Birds of Japan' (as it is, for example, in 'The Mother of the Muses'), but to accuse Harrison simply of being 'obsessive' (Forbes's word) is to dodge the challenge of each local occurrence of this extremely powerful image. In 'The Birds of Japan' the burning birds are introduced to figure the suddenness and sky-high devastation of the Hiroshima blast, then to embody the meaning of that apocalyptic event which can be comprehended only if it is fully talked (and written) about. Until that happens, optimism in life and art will be equally unjustified:

> Apostles of that pinioned Pentecaust
> of chirrupings cremated on the wing
> will have to talk their ghosts down, or we're lost.
> Until we know what they sang, who can sing?
>
> (*GG*, p. 16)

Here the Apostle/Pentecost imagery works better than in 'Snap' – partly because of the richly suggestive conflation of Pentecost and holocaust, but also because there is no distracting ambiguity about the identity of the Apostles or their task: they are those, artists and others, for whom Hiroshima represents an event-horizon for a necessary alteration of the human spirit. Poetry should play a central role in that change of consciousness, but it can do so only by following the prescription for 'survival' suggested in 'The Poetry

Lesson'. Like the Peruvian *Flambeau* and Brazilian Blue Fritillary butterflies, poetry must be ready to find sustenance – inspiration, language, shape – in the least appetising circumstances. Whether 'monster's eye' or human shit, poetry ('fine words') must learn to live off either, or both. Such an unsqueamish public stance for poetry is one that Harrison has developed, since *Anno Forty Two*, in a number of uncompromisingly political interventions. Most of them, up to late 1992, were collected by Bloodaxe as *The Gaze of the Gorgon*. As well as the title film-poem, broadcast by the BBC in September 1992, the collection includes all seven of the *Anno Forty Two* sonnets, plus 'The Morning After, I and II' (also in *SP*, pp. 157–8), 'The Mother of the Muses' and twelve additional poems, among them two poems on the Gulf War that had originally been published separately in *The Guardian* (on 5 and 18 March 1991) and then together as *A Cold Coming* by Bloodaxe Books later the same year.[1]

Both Gulf War poems address the horrors of that conflict, but in different ways. 'Initial Illumination' relates the beleaguered present day to the Anglo-Saxon past via the Farne Island cormorants that Harrison sees from a train as he travels from Newcastle to Scotland. The 'initial I' which Eadfrith, illuminator of the Anglo-Saxon Bible, decorated with cormorants is also the first-person I/eye of the poet who sees the Northumbrian coastline and is also witness to a brutal world order which makes him 'doubtful, in these dark days, what poems can do . . .'. The nature of that world order is starkly obvious in the rhetoric of the Pentagon as it once again invokes religion to justify its massive military aggression against Iraq. The much-trumpeted 'victory' of America and its allies leaves nothing but a trail of incineration and pollution behind it; even the cormorants are 'slack-necked' from the oil-clogged waters of the Gulf. The only weak point in the poem's design is its momentary lapse into the most banal of platitudes at a moment when the intricately wrought imagery could most have been trusted to enforce the required moral judgement:

> . . . let them remember, all those who celebrate,
> that their good news is someone else's bad
> or the light will never dawn on poor Mankind.
>
> (*GG*, p. 46)

Though 'good news' (Gospels) and 'light . . . dawn' are related to the poem's core imagery, their primary purpose is to solder on to the poem's powerful leitmotivs a piece of overt moralising as heavy-handed as it is unnecessary.

'A Cold Coming' is in the form of a *v.*-like dialogue, though here the poet's interlocutor is a hideously burned Iraqi soldier whose photograph – one of the most disturbing of the whole war – is used on the cover of the Bloodaxe edition (1991) of both *Guardian* poems. Where 'Initial Illumination' weaves its images together through a solid block of alternately rhymed lines, 'A Cold Coming' treks relentlessly forward by means of rhymed couplets, each one a separate stanza. The dogged momentum of a long sequence of two-line steps is perfect for the poem's insistence on facing uncomfortable truths. The first of these truths is the image of the soldier himself, incinerated to a ragged skeleton behind the wheel of his vehicle. His grisly mimicry of life is converted by Harrison into an eloquent plea to be recorded for posterity, so he speaks his thoughts into a tape-recorder. The key trope of frozen sperm is introduced with the soldier's first 'recorded' words, the 'three wise Marines' taking the place of Eliot's Magi and their 'coming' typifying not reverence or respect for life, but an arrogant desire to cheat death privately while inflicting it on a huge scale publicly. Such an option was not available to the Iraqi soldier, whose death put paid to any chance of fatherhood for him. Destroyed by superior technology and hidden behind the crass triumphalism of tabloid headlines, the soldier is the spectre not allowed to join the feast as the 'semen-bankers' return home to procreate in the usual way. Harrison is asked to lie on the soldier's behalf, pretending that he is reconciled to his own fate and to the atrocities committed by both sides in the conflict:

> Lie and pretend that I excuse
> my bombing by B52s,
>
> pretend I pardon and forgive
> that they still do and I don't live,
>
> pretend they have the burnt man's blessing
> and then, maybe, I'm spared confessing

that only fire burnt out the shame
of things I'd done in Saddam's name,

the deaths, the torture and the plunder
the black clouds all of us are under.

Say that I'm smiling and excuse
the Scuds we launched against the Jews.

(*GG*, p. 53)

Thus Harrison widens the scope of his condemnation in a morally
valid and understandable way, but at the cost of blunting the poem's
rhetorical edge. By so strongly insisting on the soldier's complicity
in the war's horrors, and thus avoiding charges of simple anti-
Americanism, Harrison turns the end of the poem into an anodyne
plea for global peace: 'Mankind' will remain 'on the rocks' (both
foundered and frozen) 'until the World renounces War', a statement
as limply unchallenging as the 'poor Mankind' section of 'Initial
Illumination'. The imbalance of politico-military *power*, so crucial
at the beginning of the poem, now gets lost in a plague-on-both-
your-houses pacifism. America's abject failure to live up to its own
vaunted self-image as world peacekeeper is simply equated with
Iraq's invasion of Kuwait, its missiles no more or less culpably
used than those of Iraq in this 'Cruise/Scud cursed millennium'.
The 'cold spunk' that was at first an image of superpower hubris
now becomes a potential Second Coming ('bottled Bethlehem') of
offspring untainted by war. In the meantime, the tape-recorder
is rewound and the poem ends with the possibility of an endless
reprise of the soldier's words. The circularity suggested by the last
stanza is a rueful acknowledgement of the need to go on repeating
the anti-war message until it is heeded – which may mean for
ever.

The first in a trio of poems inspired by air travel is 'Listening to
Sirens', in which air-raid sirens, a grim reminder of war, become
the siren-song to which Harrison creatively listens. Unlike the 'pale
Geordies' who fly south for a holiday, Harrison must remember
the 'dark winter' of Northern urban impoverishment from which
they are trying to escape. In an earlier chapter I remarked on
the importance of 'facing North' to Harrison's vision (p. 100);

'Listening to Sirens' confirms that centrality as surely as does *v*. A sustained – let alone militant – attentiveness to collective suffering can be managed only if the 'blue and bright light' of the South which dazzles the Geordie holidaymakers is refused in favour of the Northern 'dark'. In that gloomy but indispensable medium Harrison can be 'oblivious' in a way that is socially highly alert.

In 'The Act' Harrison is on an early-morning flight from Belfast to Newcastle with a group of drunken soldiers on leave. Despite their yobbish behaviour and the sexist obscenities with which their conversation is peppered, Harrison asks: 'Who am I to censure or condemn?' He confesses to having 'roistered' in similar 'male packs' himself; and he is therefore able to sympathise with the squaddies' need to kick over the traces when they are let loose for a few days from the discipline of army life: 'they want to disobey/ because they bow to orders every day'. Their rowdiness, disregard for safety regulations and 'crude repartee' ('The stewardesses clearly hate this run') are briefly contextualised as a product of the mass unemployment which has forced many Scots and Geordies into the army as a last resort.

The Prevention of Terrorism Act which gives the poem its title requires travellers to England from Northern Ireland to complete a form with details of their 'profession; place of birth; purpose of visit'. Under 'profession' Harrison (as always) puts 'poet', while reflecting on the probable response to this of the soldier in the next seat:

> The rowdy squaddy, though he doesn't know it
> (and if he did he'd brand the freak a 'queer')
> is sitting next to one who enters 'poet'
> where he puts 'Forces' . . .
>
> (*GG*, p. 20)

Though he admits to not liking the idea of 'these lads manning blocks' in Ulster, Harrison also remembers how 'alert' they appeared when 'khakied up, not kaylied', as he was driven to the airport. Whether the men have been brutalised and whether they should be patrolling the streets of Belfast at all are questions left unasked. However, Harrison is sure enough of one thing to state it to his two fellow-poets, the poem's dedicatees: 'They won't read what we three write' (*GG*, p. 21). The squaddies' indifference to what the poets write is not simply a reprise of the skinhead's attitude in *v.*: there the reaction was anger at what was seen as Harrison's class treachery. The squaddies are a more typical example of how young men in the skinhead's situation might plausibly think and act. Far from being articulate rebels, they are terrifying examples of how the sensibilities of the working-class male can be triply blunted – by proletarian machismo, by unemployment and by the routine brutalities of army life, especially in a neocolonial context. Harrison describes their behaviour unflinchingly. It is the significance of that behaviour which he fails to examine, stopping at the point where embarrassment or irritation might modulate into a genuine engagement with what has made these men what they are, and whose interests are served by their staying that way.

The sense of history, its pressures and power relations, so forcefully employed in the early 'School of Eloquence' sonnets and still present, though in a weaker form, in *v.*, is almost entirely absent here: its only glimmer of an appearance is in the reference to industrial decline and unemployment. Harrison's farewell to his 'Ulster poet friends' is an abrupt retreat from the soldiers' macho boasting: he wishes them both 'pleasures with no rough strife, no iron gates,/ and letter boxes wide enough for books'. The echo of Marvell is decisive, for 'To His Coy Mistress' is the poem *par excellence* of a willed assertion of private pleasure over social responsibility. The catch is – and always was – that Marvell's *carpe diem* appeal to the woman actually serves the institutionalised exploitation of women by men. In the same way, Harrison's rueful wish for his friends is, by its attempted evasion of the life-and-death realities of Ulster, an ironic (though largely unintended) reminder of how inescapable the 'rough strife' really is. And it is doubly ironic that the wished-for 'pleasures' are of the very sort (sexual success with women) that the squaddies were anticipating in a more straightforward way: 'fantastic fucks!'. What might have been a powerful critique of exploitation – of working-class men by the ruling class; of women by men – thus becomes an implicit acceptance that men are really all lads together.

A more assured political poem is the last in the air-travel trio, 'Y'. Here the epigraph from Margaret Thatcher ('I'm good with curtains') furnishes the central metaphor for the way in which class distinctions are nakedly exposed in the USA and discreetly concealed in Britain. The final point is concisely summed up: whatever the airline, airport or – by extension – country, 'things are going to stay/ just as they are' (*GG*, p. 23). The only consolation for the persistence of such inequality is the thought that in most plane-crash nose-dives it is the lowest-class passengers, those 'Ys in the tail', who stand the best chance of survival. Nevertheless, plane crashes do not happen often, and when they do the chances of survival are not particularly good for anyone. Even as a metaphor for economic decline and social upheaval, there is little comfort for history's steerage passengers in this unlikely scenario. Meanwhile, curtained or not, divisions of wealth and privilege will go on.

John Betjeman's comfortably nostalgic autobiographical poem provides the ironic title of 'Summoned by Bells'. Harrison's quiet is invaded not by the church bells that once called the faithful to prayer, but by the security alarms that signal a contemporary substitute for religion. Consumerism and its attendant crimes have created an obsession with protecting property, a collective neurosis that has turned the whole nation into 'one great Neighbourhood Watch'. The 'botched civilization' of which Ezra Pound complained in 'Hugh Selwyn Mauberley' (1920) has not put an end to literature, but the thief who stole Harrison's bag, only to get 'deeply pissed' at the discovery that it contained fifty copies of his latest book of poetry, is symptomatic of the irrelevance of poetry rather than its extinction. Harrison can use the thief to illustrate his own 'alarm' at the state of society, but the final irony is that the resulting poem is itself a symptom of the irrelevance it is about: it can no more be read or understood by the thief it describes than Harrison can become 'the poet my father reads' in 'The Rhubarbarians, II' (*SP*, p. 114).

'Fire & Ice' commemorates the death of the last 'dusky' in Florida. The bird's extinction and the preservation of its genes on ice link two of Harrison's most pervasive image-themes. Bird associations – of freedom, naturalness and spontaneous self-expression – are grimly poised between the lethal alternatives of 'freezered' suspension on the one hand and 'charred' (nuclear) annihilation on the other. It is a pairing as gruesome as the frozen sperm and blackened corpse in 'A Cold Coming'. (Another, more fortunate, bird (a siskin) turns up a few pages later at the beginning of 'Losing Touch', a short meditation on the importance of contact in human relations.)

After the frozen genes of 'Fire & Ice', an entirely different sense of icing is introduced in 'The Icing Hand', a new 'School of Eloquence' sonnet about Harrison senior. The father's skilful icing of cakes that will quickly be demolished at wedding receptions is compared with his lack of concern at the destruction of his carefully built seaside sandcastles by the incoming tide. As he tries to write about his father, Harrison feels his hand guided by the dead man's patient skill. Like his father, he must accept the impermanence of life, even of art; but it is that acceptance itself that gives a Keatsian intensity to the wave-on-wave, eleven-syllable inundation of the poem's finale: 'and first, ebbing, salts, then, flowing, floods this line'.

In Harrison's continuing argument with the world's zealots and life-deniers, 'The Pomegranates of Patmos', 'The Blasphemers' Banquet' and 'The Gaze of the Gorgon' are three large and ambitious contributions. The last two were broadcast on BBC television in 1989 and 1992 respectively, adding to a body of film-poems that already included *Arctic Paradise* (1981; *Astley*, pp. 377–81), about a Yukon fur-trapping family, and *Loving Memory* (1987), a four-part series on European cemeteries and funeral practices. Taking the non-television piece first, it is immediately obvious how much it shares with the other two in both structure and content. The basic structural principle of all three is a dialectical pairing of antagonistic forces. On the side of life in this poem is the unnamed twin brother of Prochorus, follower and amanuensis of St John. The brother straight away reveals his down-to-earth dislike of all that goes on in the cave on Patmos where The Book of Revelation is supposed to have been written. He says of Prochorus:

> He sits in a cave with his guru
> a batty old bugger called John,
> and scribbles on scrolls stuff to scare you
> while the rabbi goes rabbiting on.
> (stanza 2, *GG*, p. 28)

Prochorus is so thoroughly 'brainwashed' by John, so much at the service of a God obsessed with punishing humanity, that his family – especially the brother-narrator – can no longer communicate with him. Like the bewildered families of present-day Moonies, all the brother and mother can do is bewail the loss of Prochorus to a sect that gloats – like the born-again Ronald Reagan in the poem's epigraph – over the idea of damnation:

> he found a quotation that made his day
> and he tried to use to mar mine,
> how pomegranates would wither away
> and shrivelled grapes hang from the vine.
>
> (stanza 16)

The pomegranate, with its gem-like, succulent seeds, becomes the focus of what separates the brothers: Prochorus tries to turn it into a symbol of Armageddon; his brother sees it as a vagina 'best subjected to kisses and suction'. He forces Prochorus to retreat to his cave by the 'suckings and sensual licks' with which he eats his pomegranate. From then on the fruit becomes a source of joy and hope in a dark world: even at five-to-midnight on the Doomsday clock, there is still time to enjoy sex and all the pleasures offered by the beauty of Patmos. Prochorus's problem is precisely that 'he took leave of his senses' when he became fixated on the prospect of divine retribution. St John's Doomsday pessimism is as dangerous as it ever was, especially as the modern pollution of places like Patmos offers an easy warrant for gloom about the future. Against such world-weariness, the brother offers his own 'vaccine', a song whose 'six verses but seven refrains' cleverly mimics and mocks the numerology of Revelation. His answer to the puritans and apocalypse-mongers takes us back to the beleaguered celebrations of love and lovemaking in 'Following Pine' and 'Cypress and Cedar', and back further still to the unrepentant randiness of the White Queen and the PWD Man. Cunnilingus and fucking will keep Armageddon at bay: 'The stars won't fall/ nor will the fig', as long as the appetite for life remains strong enough.

A similar fierce delight in what can be wrested from life in the teeth of fanaticism is also central to 'The Blasphemers' Banquet'. Organising the film-poem around a banquet in a Bradford Indian restaurant enabled Harrison to celebrate physical pleasure and conviviality at the same time as invoking some of literature's leading blasphemers in support of Salman Rushdie. The name of the restaurant, the 'Omar Khayyam' (which the owners were about to change when filming began), was a perfect cue for the imaginary gathering of dissidents. Voltaire, Molière, Byron and Omar Khayyam himself are marshalled against Ayatollah Khomeini's intolerant pronouncements, especially the notorious *fatwa* that sent Rushdie into hiding. But the most powerful antidote to such precisian rigidity is the muck and muddle of life itself, represented in the film-poem by shots of ruined churches, abandoned graveyards and obscene graffiti. The recalcitrance of everyday reality is anathema to the zealots:

> The thorny whys and wherefores, awkward whences
> things that seduce or shame or shock the senses
> panic the one-book creeds into erecting
> a fence against all filth and all offences.
>
> (*Astley*, p. 401)

The lottery of life and death becomes a filmed auction that aptly figures 'the going – going – gone of everything'. As dead people's most personal possessions – a gold ring, bundles of books – are sold off or fail to sell, Harrison buys a marble bust of Voltaire, and we are reminded of the Frenchman's defence of freedom of speech. Byron's statue in Hyde Park provides a similar cue for historical reflection, this time on the outrage caused by his so-called Satanic poetry. Voltaire's voice speaks of the charges of irreligion against Molière and himself, and this then modulates into a short sequence of clips in which Ian Paisley, a rabbi and a nun voice their separate, sectarian versions of a shared intolerance. Finally, Harrison in person pays tribute to the absent Rushdie, particularly to *The Satanic Verses* for 'its brilliance and, yes, its blasphemy' (*Astley*, p. 406). Closing shots of the Omar Khayyam restaurant sign being dismantled clinch the significance of Omar's love for 'this fleeting life': it is only the 'life-denying fundamentalists' who cannot abide the ebb and flow of all things. We are left in the same position as Omar who, according to Fitzgerald, 'fell back upon today . . . as the only Ground he had got to stand upon'.[2]

To some people – myself included – the abruptness and passion of Harrison's intervention in the Rushdie debate were cause for some concern at the time. It seemed that in his eagerness to defend imaginative freedom, Harrison might have been gratuitously

insulting to the generality of Muslims who were not to be
equated with the Ayatollah, even though they were undoubtedly
angered by what they had been told was Rushdie's insult to
their prophet. Whereas references to 'the *Fatwa* Fascist' could
be easily defended, to anticipate the completion of a Bradford
mosque as a time when the 'muezzin's call sours Omar's ruby
vintage/ curdling the stomach of the currievore' (*Astley*, p.
400) seemed open to a charge of cultural insensitivity. In the heat of
that critical moment – critical as much for race-relations as for
freedom of expression – it was not surprising that such language
should disturb some who, on the issues of the *fatwa* and of
censorship, were squarely on Harrison's side.

Looked at now, the poem seems to me more controlled; the
balancing elements that were there from the start can be seen more
clearly, while the attack on fundamentalism looks less exclusively
directed at Islam and its adherents in Bradford. If pointed scorn
(twice) for the Koran's promise of paradise to men only can
be defended on its own merits, alongside it should be placed
the lambastings of Christian (Protestant and Catholic) and Jewish
bigotry and Harrison's 'unbeliever's' rejection of otherworldliness
no matter what its religious source. But perhaps the greatest
gesture of cross-cultural understanding in the whole poem is its
use of Omar Khayyam's famous quatrain, memorably imitated in
Fitzgerald's versions of the *Rubaiyat*. Harrison sustains the *a a b a*
rhyme-scheme throughout; not a single stanza deviates from the
pattern, which requires some very nifty footwork at times: 'pews . . .
Vindaloos . . . "good news" '; 'square . . . prayer . . . Voltaire';
and the delightful 'Lot 14 . . . Queen . . . guillotine'. At the same
time, the floating third-line ending allows great freedom in stressing
awkward words that might otherwise be difficult to accommodate:
'fundamentalists' (four times), 'Tandoori' (twice), 'blasphemies' and
'nothingness' all get in this way.

The chief concerns of the poems under discussion in this chapter –
pleasure versus pain; freedom versus repression; life versus death – are
those of a passionate liberal humanism which has not entirely
displaced the militant socialism of the early 'School of Eloquence'
sonnets. Rather, it has developed (through the later 'School' sonnets,
v. and 'The Lords of Life', for example) partly alongside and partly
as an alternative to the earlier perspective. There are moments when
the socialism reasserts itself very powerfully, especially in *Trackers*

and 'The Red Lights of Plenty'; but the most recent work, for all its political courage and continuing sense of history, is largely characterised by a stance that is markedly individualistic in its libertarianism. There is still an exemplary social significance in the predicament of Salman Rushdie, or in Harrison's encounters with redneck Americans and know-nothing Brits; but there is no longer the sort of interaction between public and private which can represent personal experience as profoundly political or collective experience as an imperative incitement to personal commitment. Retreat from the brutality of contemporary life and the threat of nuclear extinction is a typical response from *v.* onwards. In effect, the anarchic individualism of *The Loiners* has been given a historical dimension and a social conscience by 'The School of Eloquence', to produce a political position that can shift unpredictably between libertarian socialism at one extreme and liberal individualism at the other. 'The Gaze of the Gorgon' (the film-poem, not the whole collection) is an especially significant expression of the latter point of view; but before turning to that it will be useful to examine a recent theatre piece, *Square Rounds*.

Though obviously intended for the stage (it was first performed in October 1992 at the National Theatre), *Square Rounds* has a great deal in common with the film-poems. For all its attention-holding stage business and its use of music and song, it is very descriptive and discursive, ranging over nearly three centuries of European science and finally glancing back to ancient China with a command of history and theory that would be the envy of any Royal Institution lecturer. Throughout the play science is represented as an at first beguiling, then increasingly terrifying conjuring trick, with explosives, poison gas and guns pulled from the hat more often and more decisively than fertilisers, inhalers and synthetic dyes. One of the most excruciating of the play's ironies is that it was the British who first used human bones – preferably those of Southern Europeans – to make into phosphate fertiliser, a grisly precedent not lost on the German Liebig (*SR*, p. 17). Another is that it was the German Jew Fritz Haber, inventor of Nitrogen Fixation and the life-saving Methane Gas Detector, who also helped to create TNT and who developed the sort of poison gas with which Jews were to be slaughtered in the death-camps a generation later. The message is clear: when science and technology are applied to warfare, there is an inevitable, unstoppable escalation of destructive power. Even beneficial discoveries, like fertilisers and dyes, can be quickly converted to humanly disastrous ends, once racism and nationalism enter the equation. Clara Haber's tragic suicide is the only effective opting-out of this escalation by any of the play's principal characters.

In terms of the political spectrum identified above, the perspective that dominates *Square Rounds* is clearly the embattled, minimally hopeful, liberal humanism we are already familiar with from *v.* Taking a further cue from 'The Poetry Lesson', Harrison's words are browsing on shit, even if they cannot manage to 'drain the monster's duct' (*GG*, p. 17). It is a position which it is difficult not to respect, when one thinks at all – as the play insists we do – about the scientific atrocities of this century. If there is a difficulty with this point of view in the play, it is that it does not receive as powerful a formal expression as it deserves. The need to summarise large chunks of history, biography and scientific knowledge sometimes leads Harrison into irritating hyper-ingenuity, or journeyman stuff like:

It's a nutritional fact we need to extract
our nitrogen out of the ground.
There's plenty up there all about in the air
but down here not enough to go round.

And so I am afraid we're dependent for aid
on legumes like the pea and the bean
and the nitrates they give to ensure that we live
get flushed away in dung and urine.

(*SR*, p. 14)

Even allowing for the thin vein of humour that runs through Liebig's overlong speech, these lines are pretty dire. The last line in particular is exemplary in the ineptness of its metre and rhyme. Luckily, the play offers some instances of a standard against which such flops can be judged. Haber's description of the first-ever gas attack is wonderfully evocative. The lack of punctuation allows the syntax to meander from line to line in a brilliant enactment of the gas's serpentine spread:

> Lacework lassoos on the springtime April breeze
> wafted through the Maxim-shattered trees
> that this spring won't see bud or put out leaves
> and curled round the trunks like handkerchiefs.
> And then the doldrums of trench warfare broke
> when I cast over it my chlorine cloak.
>
> (*SR*, p. 49)

There are also some clever Brechtian touches at the beginning, where attention is comically drawn to the play's linguistic artifice. Haber insists that there must be 'a rhyme on every line' (p. 5) and Liebig congratulates himself on achieving 'three rhymes in a row/ . . . in a lingo I don't know' (p. 12).

A variety of 'voices' has often been present in Harrison's work, not just the plays. There are several speakers in *The Loiners* and the 'School of Eloquence' sonnets contain many bits of writing and speech by historical characters as well as Harrison's mother and father. The skinhead in *v.* has a particularly strident voice – challenging and finally supporting Harrison's own – as has the redneck neighbour in 'The Lords of Life'. Equally effective, in a quieter key, are the words of the dead Iraqi soldier in 'A Cold Coming'; and, of course, whole long poems, from 'The White Queen' to 'The Pomegranates of Patmos', can be sustained in a single impersonated vocal register.

Square Rounds strikes me as at least as much like a polyphonic poem as a verse play. The awkwardness of which some people complained in its staging would have been avoided if it had been conceived and produced as a film-poem in which visual images (battlefields, laboratories, archive footage and photographs of all sorts) could have been combined with the voices to focus intensively on the issues addressed, without the need to create stage presences, let alone 'characters', even in a Brechtian way. Quite a lot of the summarising and explaining done by the characters themselves could then have been taken over by a narrator (Harrison himself), with scope for greater freedom in drawing parallels and pointing out ironies. The versatility of a structure governed by a single voice, but into which other voices intrude or are invited, can be seen in 'The Blasphemers' Banquet'. It is just as effective in 'The Gaze of the Gorgon'.

One of three epigraphs to 'The Gaze of the Gorgon' is Nietzsche's comment, from *The Birth of Tragedy*, that 'Art forces us to gaze into the horror of existence, yet without being turned to stone.' Some of the horrors that come within the film-poem's gaze are 'ghettos, gulags, genocide', rampant materialism, poverty, drug-addiction, militarism and racism. It is a formidable tally, put together with an unflinching eye for historical and contemporary evidence. Confronting such horrors is art's Nietzschean antidote to the Gorgon's gaze which has dehumanised so many millions of people – both victims and victimisers – in the twentieth century.

Heinrich Heine's is the voice through which most of the poem is delivered. From the grand statues of Goethe and Schiller, the camera shifts to Heine's much smaller and less prominent one. He then begins a survey of his times and ours which will continue to the end of the film-poem. This formal strategy works far better than most of the historical and (auto)biographical speeches in *Square Rounds*. One reason is that the voice behind the 'voice' is very obviously Harrison's own – not just because it is him we hear on the soundtrack, but because the feeling and ideas are his as well: it is his fierce loyalty to the depreciated Jewish poet and his anger at what modern Germany has become that energise the language:

> Your average Frankfurt-am-Mainer
> doesn't give a shit for Heine,
> (nor come to that the young mainliner!).
> So elbowed to one side back here
> surrounded by junked junkies' gear
> I, Heinrich Heine, have to gaze
> on junkies winding tourniquets
> made from the belt out of their jeans,
> some scarcely older than their teens.
>
> (*GG*, p. 61)

Heine became an exile from Germany for the last twenty-five years of his life, preferring Paris, with its hopes of revolution, to the frustration of staying in his native land. It is therefore an irony – one that Heine would have grimly appreciated – that his statue should have ended up in Frankfurt to witness the daily hopelessness of the city's junkies, and to be spattered with blood from their fumbled shoot-ups. Heine himself was increasingly dependent on drugs in · his last, painful years: his poem 'Morphine' expresses his gratitude for the temporary relief they brought him. Faced with the wrecked lives of Frankfurt's addicts, Heine is forced to wonder whether art itself might become 'just another form of dope' (p. 62), if it cannot meet the creative challenge of the worst of contemporary social life. Dope it certainly *has* become for the well-heeled opera-goers who pass by the junkies on the way to their 'fix of *Figaro*' (p. 63). Amid the opaque glass towers of 'Bankfurt', art is commodified as just another object of addictive consumption; and the opera crowd is as indifferent to this abuse of wealth as was the New York Met Set in 'Oh, Moon of Mahagonny'. Heine was familiar with an exactly similar situation. From his mattress-grave ('Matrazengruft') in Paris, he took his leave of life with a poem ('Der Scheidende') that contrasts his own hard-won resignation to death, the culmination of a stormy life, with the self-satisfied materialism of a German public ('Mein liebes deutsches Publikum') that prefers its food and drink to the challenge – let alone the torments – of creativity.

Harrison could not have chosen a more congenial fellow poet than Heine to articulate his criticisms of contemporary German (and ECU-dominated European) life. The two poets have several vital things in common. Both experienced the shock of early cultural transplantation, Harrison from one class to another; Heine from one religion (Judaism) to another (Protestant Christianity). Both draw heavily on their familiarity with contrasting national ways of life – Harrison as transatlantic commuter, Heine as *émigré* in Paris. Both combine intense pleasure in the life of the senses with a baleful eye for society's follies and crimes. Both are the enemies above all of those who would stifle freedom of expression. (And, it must be added, though both pay tribute to women on occasions, neither can get beyond a limiting masculine conception of what sort of people women really are.)

A marble statue of Heine was taken to Corfu in 1892 by the art-loving Empress Elizabeth of Austria, to be given pride of place in a garden presided over by Apollo and the Muses. Ten years later, after Elizabeth's assassination in 1899, Kaiser Wilhelm II took over the property and proceeded to convert it into a mirror of his own strutting nationalism and militarism. Ernst Herter's statue of the dying Achilles, which depicts the Homeric character as 'helpless, unheroic, dying' (p. 67), did not conform to the Kaiser's idea of military power. His preference was for the armoured 'monster' (p. 69) of Johannes Götz, which he commissioned and which bore his inscription: 'The greatest German to the greatest Greek'. With the camera's help, Harrison directs our attention to the hornets that have nested in this statue's crotch:

> Envenomed hordes have gone and built
> their teeming nests in Prussia's kilt,
> and perforate the scrotal sac
> of the tutued 'Teutomaniac'.
>
> (p. 70)

A subtle and hilarious debunking is achieved in these lines. The archaic formality of 'Envenomed hordes' is promptly mocked by the demotic tone of 'have gone and built'. The statue's short tunic is similarly belittled, as a 'kilt', and "tutued 'Teutomaniac"'' gives the Prussianised superhero all the macho credibility of a paratrooper dressed as Giselle.

A lifelong republican, and a Jew into the bargain, obviously had no place in the Kaiser's garden, so Heine's statue was 'crated up and put to sea' (p. 68), arriving next in Hamburg, from whence it was later taken to Toulon in France, 'with swastikas on [its] face', after the Nazis came to power. That statue has in its hand a manuscript of 'Die Träne' ('The Tear'), one of the most famous of the *Lieder* set to music by Schumann. The whole of this song is sung to mark the transition from Frankfurt to Corfu; and its four stanzas are brilliantly imitated later when the focus shifts to the Toulon statue *in situ*. Last of the pseudo-*Lieder* stanzas is an anachronistic gesture of sympathy from Heine to the fellow-Jews who were murdered more than eighty years after his death:

> And though I gaze in sunlight
> on springtime's brightest hues,
> no longer hunted and hounded

I weep for six million Jews.

(p. 74)

Another pseudo-*Lied* occurs a little further on, near the end of the poem, after the Gorgon's gaze has been detected at work 'even in the USA' and in 'the deserts of the Gulf'. Again the tear-imagery is prominent, this time as a gesture of compassion for the victims of Desert Storm and its appalling environmental impact. The increased scope of the poem's political critique is finally consolidated by a plea, apparently by Harrison *in propria persona*, that the Toulon statue should be returned to Corfu to commemorate a meeting of European heads of state in 1994. The final irony is that that meeting is scheduled to take place in the newly restored palace of the Austrian Empress and the German Kaiser.

By marrying film-images so closely to the spoken word, with music and song as occasional further additions, Harrison has helped to revive a form pioneered in the mid 1930s by W.H. Auden and Benjamin Britten in collaboration with the film director John Grierson. (Their documentary, made for the GPO, about the night mail train from London to Glasgow, is still strikingly atmospheric.) In the 1960s and 1970s, the likes of Betjeman and Larkin had television readings of their work linked to suitable shots of Victorian architecture, Hull streets or rural churches; but this was film being used as illustration for a pre-established text. What Harrison has done is write so closely in partnership with the camera that the visual material will often dictate the direction of the verse. An example of this process was Harrison's discovery, as filming of 'The Blasphemers' Banquet' was about to start, that a Bradford church had been converted into a restaurant called the 'Omar Khayyam'. According to the film's director, Peter Symes, this accidental find set Harrison off on a new and bewildering tack:

> a further discovery of more Omar was made in the local cemetery (on a gravestone), and the film crew were treated to constant inexplicable requests to film bits of graffiti and to be sure to concentrate on 'O's' – the O on the gravestone inscription, the O of the Omar Khayyam sign as it was removed from the restaurant, the O on various

signboards. Even the director was by this time wondering where it would all end!

(*Astley*, p. 391)

Where it ended was in a series of closely connected verbal and visual variations on the O as an O-mar-like exclamation of life-affirming joy set against the levelling o-bliteration ('nothingness') wrought by death.

In 'The Gaze of the Gorgon' there is the unfolding of a pattern of connections that can only have come from Harrison following his nose – or, rather, his eye – for much of the time, allowing a sequence of discoveries to establish its own logic and momentum. More than serendipity is involved, of course; going with the flow alone could not produce the coherence or incisiveness of the finished piece. Nevertheless, Harrison's openness to the unexpected and his willingness to improvise are crucial to the shape and substance of his television pieces, as they are to those of his theatre and opera work. It is encouraging to see that at least one younger poet has taken up the challenge of working in this way. Simon Armitage's *Xanadu*, broadcast by BBC2 in June 1992, is a bruising evocation and indictment of conditions on a Rochdale council estate. Original and versatile as this piece certainly is, it would have been less likely to be commissioned, written, produced, broadcast or published (Bloodaxe, 1992) without Harrison's television work as an incitement and example.

Harrison's ability to keep extending the possibilities of the film-poem is strikingly clear in *Black Daisies for the Bride* (BBC2, 30 June 1993), where the ravages of Alzheimer's Disease, first considered in 'The Mother of the Muses', are further explored through a group of women sufferers in a Yorkshire hospital. Three of the women, with symptoms as different as their personalities, are contrasted with their younger selves as brides. Speaking and singing Harrison's verse, the actresses playing Maria Tobin, Muriel Prior and Kathleen Dickinson testify to the youthful hopes, abilities and sheer appetite for life blighted, but not totally extinguished, by the relentless progress of the disease. The patients use their own words, sounds and gestures. Everyone else in the film, including the actual nurses on Whernside Ward and an actress playing a deeply compassionate therapist, is given verse to deliver that closely mimics the popular songs and hymns whose rhythms remain somehow reachable in all but the most damaged minds. *Black Daisies for the Bride* is moving evidence that the rescuing from oblivion of individual histories is still inseparable (as it was in 'Working') from Harrison's larger historical and political concerns. In this case those larger concerns include a willingness to confront, as prelude to Alzheimer's Awareness Week, the uncomfortable reality of a disease that currently afflicts up to three-quarters of a million people in Britain.

In a generally enthusiastic review of *The Gaze of the Gorgon*, Terry Eagleton stresses both its strength and its limitation:

> There is a clenched, exposed engagement in all this work, incomparably starker and more impassioned than almost anything English poetry currently has to offer; but it is as though, in Eliot's phrase, we had the experience but missed the meaning. . . . What we expect from a Harrison is a radical rather than a liberal perspective, since we aren't likely to get it from ninety percent of his literary colleagues.[3]

The 'liberal perspective' complained of here is typified by the sort of hand-me-down generalisations about how horrible war is, and how it must stop, that I have noted above. When we encounter such facile evasions of the challenge of explanation, we realise what promise the 'clenched, exposed engagement' of Harrison's interventions has held out to us – and how difficult it is to keep fulfilling it. Like Harrison's work as a whole, *The Gaze of the Gorgon* offers a spectrum of political perspectives; but Eagleton is none the less right to point out that the best of that work, here as elsewhere, has encouraged us to expect (or at least, hope for) something from the radical end of that spectrum, even if we are sometimes disappointed.

In the opening chapter of this book I quoted Orwell's insistence that working-class writing 'can't help being . . . a literature of revolt'. Tony Harrison's poetry gives plenty of support to that claim. It also demonstrates that the 'bourgeois methods' referred to by Orwell may be so subverted as to make room not just for an explicitly proletarian content, but for a distinctively working-class appropriation of idiom and form. Each recuperation of the hidden or misrepresented history of his class is, for Harrison, an acknowledgement both of his cultural origins and of the ultimate validity of his family's limited lives. At the same time, his raids on the ruling class's rhetorical arsenal have equipped him for some full-scale onslaughts on contemporary injustices and lunacies of all sorts. These onslaughts (or 'interventions', as I call them in this chapter) offer evidence aplenty of Harrison's continuing skill in commandeering the most time-hallowed, exclusive forms for his polemical purposes. What hampers him at times are ideological contradictions which he brings with him from his class background and which find a too-easy confirmatory echo in the gender and racial stereotypes of contemporary Western culture. Challenging those falsifications of what women and men are, and are capable of, would be a welcome next step in the development of Harrison's bravely political art.

Notes

(See Bibliography for full publication details.)

CHAPTER 1

1. *The Uses of Literacy* contains no mention at all of scholarship *girls*. Not until *A Local Habitation* in 1988 is their existence recognised (e.g. on p. 156). For more details of this book, see Note 23 below.
2. *The Uses of Literacy* (1957), Chapter X, pp. 238–49. For a full discussion of the cultural cost of the postwar selective system of education and its relevance to Harrison's work, see Ken Worpole, 'Scholarship boy: the poetry of Tony Harrison', *New Left Review* (1985), reprinted in *Astley*, pp. 61–74.
3. Hoggart (1957), p. 243.
4. *ibid.*, p. 245.
5. *ibid.*, p. 242.
6. *ibid.*, p. 244.
7. George Orwell, *Collected Essays, Journalism and Letters*, Vol. 2, (1970), p. 57.
8. *ibid.*, p. 58.
9. *ibid.*
10. The causes and consequences of this failure may be traced through the work of many sociologists, historians and cultural commentators. I have found particularly useful: Frank Parkin, *Class Inequality and Political Order* (1972); Jeremy Seabrook, *What Went Wrong?* (1978) (this is especially strong on the emotional impoverishment of postwar working-class

life); Chas Critcher, 'Sociology, cultural studies and the postwar working class', in J. Clarke, C. Critcher and R. Johnson (eds), *Working Class Culture: Studies in history and theory* (1979); Ralph Miliband, *Capitalist Democracy in Britain* (1984); Anne Phillips, *Divided Loyalties* (1987) (Phillips adds an important feminist perspective to that of class); Alan Sinfield, *Literature, Politics and Culture in Post-War Britain* (1989), especially Chapter 13, 'The Way We Live Now'.

11. See Luke Spencer, 'British working class fiction: the sense of loss and the potential for transformation', in R. Miliband, J. Panitch and J. Saville (eds), *Socialist Register 1988*, pp. 366–86.
12. Eric Homberger, *The Art of the Real* (1977), p. 209.
13. *ibid.*, p. 215.
14. Jon Silkin (ed.), *Poetry of the Committed Individual* (1973), p. 27.
15. Robert Conquest (ed.), *New Lines, 1957*, pp. xiv-xvi. Quoted by Silkin, *Poetry of the Committed Individual*, p. 17.
16. See G.S. Fraser, *The Modern Writer and His World* (1964), p. 321.
17. The word was first used in this precise sense by A. Alvarez in 'Beyond the gentility principle', his introduction to *The New Poetry* (1962 and many editions since).
18. Douglas Dunn, 'The Grudge', *Stand* (1975), pp. 4–6.
19. *ibid.*, p. 5.
20. *ibid.*, p. 6.
21. *ibid.*
22. *Where I Used to Play on the Green* (1982), *The Hawthorn Goddess* (1984) and *The Rape of the Rose* (1987).
23. Richard Hoggart, *A Local Habitation: Life and times, Volume 1: 1918–1940* (1988), p. 55.
24. Raymond Williams, 'The tenses of the imagination', *Writing in Society* (1983), p. 261.
25. Antony Easthope, *Poetry as Discourse* (1983), pp. 67, 68, 69.
26. *ibid.*, p. 76.
27. *ibid.*
28. Published in *Critical Quarterly*, Vol. 28, No. 3, pp. 69–70. It has not, so far as I know, been reprinted anywhere else.

Chapter 2

1. Anne Cluysenaar, *Stand* (1970), pp. 73–4.
2. First published in 1955 and reprinted in 1966 with a 'Political Preface' that unequivocally aligned instinctual desublimation with radical social action: 'Today the fight for life, the fight for Eros, is the *political* fight' (Beacon Press edition, p. xxv).
3. *Eros and Civilization*, pp. 87–8. Marcuse goes on to argue, in his *One-Dimensional Man* (1964), that the false desublimation offered by such things as pornography only serves the ends of social subordination. It is a way of keeping people 'happily' in line.
4. *Eros and Civilization*, p. 236.
5. *ibid.*, p. 235.
6. Ronald Hyam, *Britain's Imperial Century 1815–1914* (1976), pp. 135 ff.
7. Like Lowell, Harrison has adopted Andrew Marvell's eight-line stanza of rhymed couplets with eight syllables to the line, but his iambic rhythm is much closer to the regularity of the Marvellian model (e.g. 'The Garden') than are Lowell's enormously varied measures. Thematically, Harrison is attempting something akin to Lowell's sad contemplation of a world out of love with itself.
8. 'Elegy 19: To His Mistress Going To Bed'.
9. A recent commentator (male) has said that women 'are much celebrated in [Harrison's] work' (Jonathan Barker, 'Peru, Leeds, Florida, Keats', in *Astley*, p. 47). This is certainly true; but there is a remarkable reluctance, even among female commentators (*Astley, passim*), to ask precisely what it is about women that Harrison likes so much. A refreshing exception is Marilyn Hacker who identifies the 'masculine myopia' and 'phallocentrism' in Harrison's early poetry, though she is too ready to claim the absence of it in 'The School of Eloquence' and later work (*Astley*, pp. 252–3).

Chapter 3

1. Harrison's other, occasional non-theatrical verse translations include the three original 'Travesties' (*L*, pp. 31–4) and 'The Ballad of Geldshark' (*SP*, p. 104).

2. Several of the contributors in *Astley* make useful comments about the problems of translation and the specific theatrical conditions in which Harrison has worked.
3. *The Misanthrope* (1973), p. vi. Also *Astley*, p. 140.
4. *Molière: Five Plays* (1982), p. 228.
5. *Aeschylus: The Oresteian Trilogy* (1956), p. 151.
6. *The Orestes Plays of Aeschylus* (1962), p. 164.
7. Richard Beadle (ed.), *The York Plays* (1982). All quotations from the York Cycle texts are from this edition.
8. For the most readable versions of these, see *The Complete Plays of the Wakefield Master*, adapted by J. Russell Brown (1983). The complete Wakefield cycle is in Martial Rose (ed.), *The Wakefield Mystery Plays* (1961).
9. Greek tragedies like *The Oresteia* would have been first performed exclusively by men wearing masks. However, Harrison wanted to do much more than imitate archaic acting conventions: 'It's not an antiquarian concern that made me want only men in the play, it was to lock the play into an all-male statement' (*Astley*, p. 244). Harrison saw that 'statement', in which Aeschylus's notorious 'patriarchal propaganda' (*ibid.*) is given maximum force, as a way of challenging the modern audience's view of gender relations. He admits that that aim was not fully realised, but only – in his opinion – because the production did not put even *more* emphasis on the unequal battle of the sexes: 'Our production should have got that abrasion right, and if I had managed to prevail upon them to segregate men and women in the audience more of it would have happened' (*Astley*, p. 245). For further comment on *Square Rounds*, see pp. 127–30.
10. See Chapter 2, Note 9 above.
11. This comment was made to John Haffenden during an interview (quoted in Note 9 above) first published in *Poetry Review* (January 1984) and reprinted in *Astley*, pp. 227–46. The comment is on p. 241.

CHAPTER 4

1. E.P. Thompson, *The Making of the English Working Class* (1963), p. 174.

2. Tidd's words are quoted by Thompson in *ibid.*, p. 716.

3. A more exhaustive reading of this poem as 'a *bricolage* of international elements, using techniques of intertextual allusion, punning, self-conscious analogy and juxtaposition' may be found in Rick Rylance, 'Tony Harrison's Languages', in Antony Easthope and John O.Thompson *Contemporary Poetry Meets Modern Theory* (eds.), (1991), pp. 53–67. The same article appears, virtually unchanged, in *Astley*, pp. 114–28.

4. 'Social Mobility' makes a similar point more succinctly: 'Ah, the proved advantages of scholarship!/ Whereas his dad took cold tea for his snap,/ he slaves at nuances, knows at just one sip/ *Château Lafite* from *Châteauneuf du Pape.*' As well as Harrison's own situation, this could apply to other wine-loving intellectuals from working-class families like Lord (Roy) Jenkins, whose father (unlike Harrison's) *was* a miner. Unfortunately, the thing is so glibly done that it invites the obvious retort that the wine will taste no worse for such self-mockery! Indeed, the danger is rather that the self-mockery may be savoured as pleasurably as the wine.

5. Desmond Graham, review of *From 'The School of Eloquence' and other poems, Stand*, Vol. 20, No.4 (1979), p. 79.

6. Thompson, *The Making of the English Working Class*, pp. 334–5.

7. Marcuse, *Eros and Civilization* (1966), p. 232.

8. Bruce Woodcock sees the reference to Burke as exemplifying only 'the imperative to translate potentially explosive content into a nicely turned form' ('Classical vandalism: Tony Harrison's invective', *Critical Quarterly* (1990), p. 57). I hope my own comments indicate clearly enough why such a view neglects the full irony of the situation Harrison depicts.

9. Daniel Jones, *An English Pronouncing Dictionary* (1917; 10th edition, London, 1949). Among his other works in this field is *An Outline of English Phonetics* (6th edition, New York, 1948).

10. Harrison's word perhaps owes something to William Cobbett's nonce-word 'Heddekashun', for a definition of which see his *Cottage Economy* (1850). Compare the ingenious 'revurlooshun-airy vurse' of 'The Ballad of Babelabour' (*SP*, p. 103).

11. Hoggart, *The Uses of Literacy* (1957), p. 241.

12. Richard Johnson notes the family-based character of radical education during this period: 'The distinctive feature was, at

first sight, an emphasis upon informing mature understandings
and upon the education of men and women as adult citizens
of a more just social order. But radicals were also concerned
with men and women as educators of their own children
and they improvised forms for this task too. It might,
however, be truer to say that the child–adult distinction
was itself less stressed in this tradition, or in parts of it,
than in the contemporary middle-class culture of childhood.'
' "Really useful knowledge": radical education and working
class culture, 1790–1848', in Clarke, Critcher and Johnson
(1979), p. 77.

13. Hoggart, *The Uses of Literacy*, p. 241.
14. *Palladas: Poems*, p. 9.
15. Blake Morrison, 'The filial art: a reading of contemporary
    British poetry' (1987), p. 192. The section on Harrison is also
    in *Astley*, pp. 54–60.
16. Morrison, 'The Filial Art', p. 193.
17. In 'Clearing, I' he says of the family home: 'A stammerer died
    here and I believe/ this front room with such ghosts taught me
    my trade.' This certainly does not much resemble the cheerless,
    silent front room of 'Study', in which the only inspiration
    comes from *Aeneid VI*, certainly not from the family deaths.
18. See pp. 27–8 above
19. Morrison, 'The Filial Art' (1987) and *Astley*. See note 15 above.

CHAPTER 5

1. Bruce Woodcock summarises some very sharp comments on
   the portrayal of the skinhead. They come from a group of
   'young unemployed people', among them an 'ex-NF, ex-
   skinhead'. ('Classical vandalism: Tony Harrison's invective',
   Critical Quarterly (1990) p. 61).
2. 'Home, home to my woman' comes at the beginning of two
   successive stanzas, and the Berg opera to which Harrison
   and his 'woman' listen is *Lulu*. According to Bernard
   O'Donoghue, this is a 'scenario which expresses the roles of
   the female in Harrison's work with caustic deftness' (*Astley*,
   p. 259). O'Donoghue is carefully hedging his bets, neither
   quite praising Harrison for 'caustically' exposing his view of

women, nor quite condemning him for the narrowness of that view itself. A sounder judgement of the poem's 'masculine ethos' may be found in Woodcock, 'Classical vandalism' (pp. 61–2), where Harrison's voice and that of the skinhead are found to be complicit in denigrating both women and 'cissy' men.

CHAPTER 6

1. An early, equally sardonic use of the cornucopia image is in '"Flying down to Rio"': A Ballad of Beverly Hills': 'Big mouth of the horn of plenty/ horny horny Hollywood' (*SP*, p. 105). Note also the American context.

CHAPTER 7

1. Harrison was not the only poet to respond to events in Kuwait and Iraq. Some other hard-hitting interventions may be found in *Poetry Review* (Summer 1992), which begins with a twenty-five-page section ('A Hundred Harms') on the Gulf War. Especially powerful are Jo Shapcott's 'Phrase Book' and the two poems by Helen Dunmore, one of which refers to the same Iraqi soldier whose charred body figures so prominently in 'A Cold Coming': 'That killed head straining through the windscreen/ with its frill of bubbles in the eye-sockets/ is not trying to tell you something –/ it is telling you something.' ('Poem on the Obliteration of 100,000 Iraqi Soldiers')
2. Preface to *The Rubaiyat of Omar Khayyam*, transl. Edward Fitzgerald (1974), p. 22.
3. 'Metre v. madness', *Poetry Review* (Winter 1992/3), p. 54.

Bibliography

(The following texts are those that have helped to shape and/or support what is said in this study. The list does not include texts already identified in Abbreviations and Chronology.)

Alvarez, A., *The New Poetry*, Penguin, Harmondsworth, 1962.

Aristophanes, *Lysistrata/The Acharnians/The Clouds*, transl. Alan H. Sommerstein, Penguin, Harmondsworth, 1973.

Armitage, Simon, *Xanadu*, Bloodaxe, Newcastle upon Tyne, 1992.

Astley, Neil, 'Tony Harrison: selective bibliography', *Astley*, pp. 504–11.

Barker, Jonathan, 'Peru, Leeds, Florida, Keats', *Astley*, pp. 46–53.

Beadle, Richard (ed.), *The York Plays*, Edward Arnold, London, 1982.

Brown, J. Russell, *The Complete Plays of the Wakefield Master*, Heinemann, London, 1983.

Clarke, J., Critcher, C. and Johnson, R. (eds), *Working-Class Culture: Studies in history and theory*, Hutchinson, London, 1979.

Cluysenaar, Anne, Review of *The Loiners*, *Stand*, vol. 12, no. 1, 1970, pp. 73–4.

Crucefix, Martyn, 'The weed and the rose', *Poetry Review*, vol. 82, no. 1, 1992, pp. 21–2.

Dunmore, Helen, 'Poem on the Obliteration of 100,000 Iraqi Soldiers', *Poetry Review*, vol. 82, no. 2, 1992, p. 10.

Dunn, Douglas, 'The Grudge', *Stand*, vol. 16, no. 4., 1975, pp. 4–6.

Dunn, Douglas, 'Formal Strategies in Harrison's Poetry', *Astley*, pp. 129–32.

Dunn, Douglas, ' "Importantly Live": Harrison's Lyricism', *Astley*, pp. 254–7.

Eagleton, Terry, 'Antagonisms: v.', *Poetry Review*, vol. 76, nos 1 & 2, 1986; *Astley*, pp. 348–50.

Eagleton, Terry, 'Metre v. madness', *Poetry Review*, vol. 82, no. 4, 1992/3, pp. 53–4.

Easthope, Antony, *Poetry as Discourse*, Methuen, London, 1983.

Easthope, Antony and Thompson, John O., *Contemporary Poetry Meets Modern Theory*, Harvester Wheatsheaf, Hemel Hempstead, 1991.

Fitzgerald, Edward (transl.), *The Rubaiyat of Omar Khayyam*, Garnstone Press, London, 1974.

Forbes, Peter, 'The bald eagles of Canaveral', *Astley*, pp. 486–95.
Forbes, Peter (ed.), *Poetry Review*, vol. 82, no. 2, Summer 1992 (the Gulf War number).
Forbes, Peter, Review of *The Gaze of the Gorgon*, *The Guardian*, 27 October, 1992, G2 section, p. 11.
Fraser, G.S., *The Modern Writer and his World*, Penguin, Harmondsworth, 1964.
Garofalakis, Mary, 'The American versus/verses', *Astley*, pp. 331–7.
Graham, Desmond, Review of *Palladas: Poems*, *Stand*, vol. 17, no. 3, 1976, pp.75–6.
Graham, Desmond, Review of *From 'The School of Eloquence' and other poems*, *Stand*, vol. 20, no. 4, 1979, pp. 79–80.
Grant, Damian, 'The voice of history in British poetry, 1970–84', *Études Anglaises*, XXXVIII, no. 2, 1985, pp. 158–79. An extended version of the section on Harrison is in *Astley*, pp. 104–13.
Gunn, Thom, 'The unsettled motorcyclist's vision of his death', *The Sense of Movement*, Faber & Faber, London, 1957.
Hacker, Marilyn, 'Eloquent ingloriousness: *Selected Poems*', *The Nation*, 27 February 1988; also *Astley*, pp. 247–53.
Haffenden, John, Interview with Tony Harrison, *Poetry Review*, vol. 73, no. 4, 1984, pp. 17–30; also *Astley*, pp. 227–46.
Harrison, Tony: all major publications may be found under Abbreviations and Chronology. However, the works listed here are of interest for a variety of reasons.
'The inkwell of Dr Agrippa', *Astley*, pp. 32–5.
'Shango the Shaky Fairy', *London Magazine*, vol. 10, no. 1, April 1970, pp. 5–27; also *Astley*, pp. 88–103.
'*The Oresteia* in the making: letters to Peter Hall', *Astley*, pp. 275–80.
'Prologue' (poem), *Critical Quarterly*, vol. 28, no. 3, 1986, pp. 69–70.
'Facing up to the Muses', Presidential Address to the Classical Association, April 1988. Published in *Proceedings of the Classical Association*, 85 (1988) and in *Astley*, pp. 429–54.
Heine, Heinrich, *Selected Verse*, ed. and transl. Peter Branscombe, Penguin, Harmondsworth, 1968.
Hoggart, Richard, *The Uses of Literacy*, Chatto & Windus, London, 1957.
Hoggart, Richard, Interview with Tony Harrison, *Astley*, pp. 36–45.
Hoggart, Richard, *A Local Habitation: Life and Times, Volume 1: 1918–1940*, Chatto & Windus, London, 1988.
Homberger, Eric, *The Art of the Real*, Dent, London, 1977.
Hyam, Ronald, *Britain's Imperial Century 1815–1914*, Batsford, London, 1976.
Johnson, R., ' "Really useful knowledge": radical education and working-class culture, 1790–1848', J. Clarke, C. Critcher, and R. Johnson (eds), *Working-Class Culture: Studies in history and theory*, Hutchinson, London, 1979, pp. 75–102.
Kustow, Michael, 'Where Yorkshire grit meets Attic wit', *The Guardian*, 1 October 1992, p. 25.

Larrissy, Edward, *Reading Twentieth Century Poetry*, Basil Blackwell, Oxford, 1990.

Lennon, Peter, 'The world seen from the gods', *The Guardian*, 19 March 1990, p. 21.

Levi, Peter, 'Pagan idioms: *Palladas*', *Times Literary Supplement*, 6 February 1976; also in *Astley*, pp. 136–7.

Marcuse, Herbert, *One-Dimensional Man*, Beacon Press, Boston, MA, 1964.

Marcuse, Herbert, *Eros and Civilization*, Beacon Press, Boston, MA, 1966.

McDuff, David, Review of *Selected Poems* (1984), *Stand*, vol. 27, no. 4, 1985/6, pp.73–6.

Miliband, Ralph, *Capitalist Democracy in Britain*, Oxford University Press, Oxford, 1984.

Morrison, Blake, *The Movement*, Oxford University Press, Oxford, 1980.

Morrison, Blake, 'The filial art: A reading of contemporary British poetry', *The Yearbook of English Studies*, vol. 17, 1987, pp. 179–217. Section Three is reprinted in *Astley*, pp. 54–60.

O'Donoghue, Bernard, 'Disparate virtuosity: *Dramatic Verse: 1973–1985*', *Poetry Review*, vol. 76, no. 4, 1986, pp. 4–6; also *Astley*, pp. 258–61.

Orwell, George, *Collected Essays, Journalism and Letters, Vol. 2*, Penguin, Harmondsworth, 1970.

Parkin, Frank, *Class Inequality and Political Order*, Paladin, St Albans, 1972.

Phillips, Anne, *Divided Loyalties*, Virago, London, 1987.

Pybus, Rodney, Review of *Continuous* (1981) and *U.S. Martial* (1981), *Stand*, vol. 24, no. 2, 1983, pp. 73–5.

Raine, Craig, *Rich*, Faber & Faber, London, 1984.

Roche, Paul (transl.), *The Orestes Plays of Aeschylus*, Mentor, New York, 1962.

Rose, Martial (ed.), *The Wakefield Mystery Plays*, Evans Brothers, London, 1961.

Rylance, Rick, 'Tony Harrison's Languages', *Contemporary Poetry Meets Modern Theory*, Easthope, Antony and Thompson, John O. (eds), Harvester Wheatsheaf, Hemel Hempstead, 1991. A different version appears in *Astley*, pp. 114–28.

Seabrook, Jeremy, *What Went Wrong?*, Gollancz, London, 1978.

Seabrook, Jeremy, *Working-Class Childhood*, Gollancz, London, 1982.

Silkin, Jon (ed.), *Poetry of the Committed Individual*, Penguin, Harmondsworth, 1973.

Sinfield, Alan (ed.), *Society and Literature 1945–1970*, Methuen, London, 1983.

Sinfield, Alan, *Literature, Politics and Culture in Post-War Britain*, Basil Blackwell, Oxford, 1989.

Spencer, Luke, 'British working class fiction: the sense of loss and the potential for transformation', *Socialist Register 1988*, Miliband, R., Panitch, L. and Saville, J. (eds), Merlin, London, pp. 366–86.

Symes, Peter, 'Blasphemy and death: on film making with Tony Harrison', *Astley*, pp. 384–94.

Thompson, E.P., *The Making of the English Working Class*, Gollancz, London, 1963.

Vellacott, Philip (transl.), *Aeschylus: The Oresteian Trilogy*, Penguin, Harmondsworth, 1956.

Wilbur, Richard (transl.), *Molière: Five Plays*, Methuen, London, 1982.

Williams, Raymond, 'The tenses of the imagination', *Writing in Society*, Verso, London, 1983, pp. 259–68.

Woodcock, Bruce, 'Classical vandalism: Tony Harrison's invective', *Critical Quarterly*, vol.32, no.2, Summer 1990, pp. 50–65.

Worpole, Ken, 'Scholarship boy: the poetry of Tony Harrison', *New Left Review*, no.153, Sept./Oct. 1985, pp. 63–74. Reprinted in *Astley*, pp. 61–74.

Young, Alan, 'Weeds and white roses: the poetry of Tony Harrison', *Critical Quarterly*, vol.26, nos.1 & 2, 1984, pp. 157–63. Reprinted in *Astley*, pp. 167–73.

Index